Abner
Doubleday

Young Baseball Pioneer

Illustrated by Gray Morrow

Abner Doubleday

Young Baseball Pioneer

By Montrew Dunham

ALADDIN PAPERBACKS

First Aladdin Paperbacks edition 1995
Copyright © 1965 by the Bobbs-Merrill Company, Inc.

Aladdin Paperbacks
An imprint of Simon & Schuster Children's Publishing Division
New York, NY 10020

Printed in the United States of America
10 9 8 7 6 5 4 3 2 1

Library of Congress Cataloging-in-Publication Data
Dunham, Montrew.
Abner Doubleday, young baseball pioneer / by Montrew Dunham.
p.   cm.
"Aladdin Paperbacks."
ISBN 0-689-71788-1
1. Doubleday, Abner, 1819–1893—Juvenile literature.   2. Baseball players—United
States—Biography—Juvenile literature.
[1. Doubleday, Abner, 1819–1893.   2. Baseball players.]   I. Title.
GV865.D6D86   1995
796.357'092—dc20
[B]   93-45400

To Bob

Illustrations

Full pages

Numerous smaller illustrations

Contents

Books by Montrew Dunham

GEORGE WESTINGHOUSE: YOUNG INVENTOR

OLIVER WENDELL HOLMES, JR.: BOY OF JUSTICE

Abner

Doubleday

Young Baseball Pioneer

A Famous
Visitor

ABNER Doubleday leaned against the fence post and tossed his ball into the air, then caught it without looking. He didn't watch it because he was watching his friend Charley.

Charley lived across the road from Abner in Auburn, New York, and the two boys often played ball together. Today when Abner had called his friend to play, however, Charley had been too busy. He was sweeping the walk.

Abner's brother Tom had been too busy, also. Everyone in town seemed to be too busy on this last day of May, 1825.

Bright speckles of light darted about on the

grass as the sun shone through green leaves dancing in the breeze. Suddenly Abner jumped back as a long gray cat came running through the gate. Abner's dog Brownie came chasing after her.

"Brownie!" Abner shouted. "Come back!"

Brownie looked back at Abner but kept on chasing the cat.

"Oh, no!" Abner exclaimed. "Brownie, come back here!"

At that moment Tom came running from the barn. "I'm through with my chores, Abner," he called. "I can play ball now."

Abner was glad to see his brother. "I'll stand down here. You stand at the other end of the yard." He tossed the ball to Tom.

Tom caught the ball easily. "You're lucky you're only six and don't have any chores to do!" His voice rose. "Here it comes!" He threw the ball back.

Abner had to leap into the air to catch it.

The ball was lopsided. One seam was coming open and the insides were beginning to come through. Abner clasped the ball in his hands and tried to shape it round again, as he would a snowball. He leaned back and threw the ball as hard as he could.

"Ho!" Tom caught the ball easily and started to throw it back, then stopped. The stuffing of rubber strips was poking through the broken seam again. "It's hard to throw this ball straight," he said. "It's coming apart."

"I know," said Abner. "Maybe Ma will fix it. Throw it to me and I'll go see."

"It hasn't been very long since she made it." Tom pushed the stuffing in with his finger and tried to pull the shabby leather cover together. "I don't know whether she'll want to fix it or not. She's making a dress for Amanda to wear tomorrow," he said.

Abner looked across the street at Charley, who

was still sweeping the walk in front of his house. "Tom, why does Charley have to sweep the walk just because General Lafayette is coming to Auburn tomorrow?"

"I guess the whole town has to look its best," Tom answered. He looked at Charley, then shook his head and added doubtfully, "It doesn't seem like a hero like General Lafayette is going around looking at all the walks." He leaned over and rolled the ball across the grass to Abner. "Go see what Ma says. Maybe she'll fix it."

Abner ran to pick the ball up, then took it into the house. It was dark and shadowy inside after the bright outdoors. "Ma!" Abner called. "Ma, where are you?"

"Right here," his mother answered from the kitchen. "What do you want?"

By now Abner's eyes were used to the darkness. He could see his mother kneeling on the floor in the kitchen. His sister Amanda was

14

standing on a stool. Mother was pinning the hem of Amanda's new dress with pins from the pincushion on the floor beside her.

Abner ran to his mother and held the ball out. "Ma, would you sew this up again, please?"

Mother looked up at the ball but didn't take it. She went on pinning Amanda's dress.

"See, Ma, the stuffing is coming out." Abner poked his finger in the hole. "It won't throw straight."

Ma stopped just long enough to brush up the moist curling hair at her neck. She looked at Abner without a smile. "Don't make it any worse than it is."

Amanda tossed her head and smiled scornfully. "Ma doesn't have time to fix your old ball." Importantly she smoothed down the crisp ruffles of her new dress. "She has to get my dress finished for tomorrow!"

Mother gave Amanda a stern look and said

quietly, "All right, Abner, put the ball on the table. I'll try to get to it."

As Abner ran out the front door he yelled, "Tom! Tom! I think Ma will fix it!"

"Now?" Tom asked eagerly.

Abner frowned. "Probably not right now. She didn't say. She's fixing Amanda's dress."

Tom didn't wait for all of Abner's answer. He was looking down the street. "What does Mrs. Scott have?"

MRS. SCOTT AND THE BUNTING

Both boys looked to see Mrs. Scott with an armload of red, white, and blue material. She was walking so fast that it looked as if she were coming along the street on wheels.

Then the accident happened! Abner saw it coming and started to yell, but he was too late. He didn't see the cat, but when he saw Brownie running he knew the cat was coming, too. "No, Brownie, no!" he screamed, but Brownie didn't hear him. Ears laid flat and tail flying behind, Brownie ran straight in front of Mrs. Scott.

Mrs. Scott was so short and round and her bundle was so large that she never knew what made her fall, but suddenly, without warning, she sat down. The red, white, and blue material billowed in the air and settled on top of her.

Abner and Tom started to laugh. They couldn't help themselves. Then they did their best to stop laughing and rushed to help Mrs. Scott to her feet.

Brownie came running through the gate. "Aren't you ashamed of yourself, Brownie," Abner cried.

"Is that your dog?" Mrs. Scott demanded. Her face was red and her mouth was set in a straight line as she struggled to untangle herself. "Oh, dear!" She tried to brush off her dress. "Where is your Ma? Was that your dog?"

Abner smiled weakly. "We're sorry, ma'm."

"I should think you would be! A beast like that should not be permitted to run loose!" Mrs. Scott frowned and looked very cross. "Go get your Ma!"

"Yes, ma'm!" Tom was glad to run after Ma. "I'll get her."

"Abner, help me get all this bunting out of

18

the dirt," Mrs. Scott commanded. "It will be ruined! It's for the decorations at the ballroom for General Lafayette, and it will all be ruined!"

Abner helped pick up the material and brushed it off before handing it to Mrs. Scott, who rolled it up in a bundle again.

Ma rushed from the house and down the steps to the walk where Mrs. Scott was standing. "Are you all right?" she asked anxiously.

Mrs. Scott took a deep breath. "Yes, I think I am," she said, her smooth round face very serious. "But it's lucky I didn't break a leg!" She nodded toward Tom. "Did your boy tell you what happened?"

"Yes, and I'm sorry, Mrs. Scott," Ma said. "Could Tom go along to help you carry your decorations? That's a bulky load for you to handle all by yourself."

Mrs. Scott set her hat straight on her head again and pinned it firmly with a long straight pin. Her chin lifted as she took another deep breath. "Yes, he can help. Tom, take that end of the bundle." She frowned and turned to Mrs. Doubleday again. "What about that dog?"

"Abner, you go put Brownie in the barn," Ma said firmly.

"All right, Ma." Abner hesitated a moment. "Can't I go, too? I could help."

"You're not——" Mother started to say he was not big enough to help, but then she saw his eager face. She paused only a moment before saying, "Yes, Abner, you may go along to help. First, though, put Brownie in the barn. Then you may catch up with Tom and Mrs. Scott."

Abner ran back to the barn. Brownie saw him coming and wagged his tail.

"You're a bad dog!" Abner scolded. "You got us all in trouble."

Brownie's tail dropped limply and he hurried, cowering, to the barn.

"You stay in the barn till I get back!" Abner shouted. Then he wheeled and ran to catch up with Tom and Mrs. Scott.

As he came up behind Tom one end of the bunting blew free.

"Get it, Abner!" shouted Tom. "It's starting to unroll!"

Mrs. Scott looked back. "Don't you get any of that on the ground, boys!" she cried. "It's dirty enough already because of that foolish dog of yours."

Abner caught the free end, which dipped dangerously close to the ground, and gathered it in his arms. "No, ma'm, we won't!"

Mrs. Scott bustled on like a fat little hen, talking the entire way. "Oh, my, there's so much to be done! Everything has to be ready by tonight for General Lafayette's visit tomorrow." She wagged her head. "It just doesn't seem real that such a great man is coming to Auburn!"

Abner ran, trying to keep up with Tom. His face was hot and he was out of breath, but it was fun being part of all this excitement. He knew about General Lafayette's visit tomorrow because Pa had told him. Pa was editor of the newspaper, the *Cayuga Patriot*.

"Oh, my!" Mrs. Scott went on. "I do hope it doesn't rain for the parade tomorrow."

Abner looked up at the sky and frowned. How could it rain? The sky was cloudless and the sun was shining brightly. It couldn't rain!

"I hope it doesn't rain!" Mrs. Scott exclaimed again as she turned the corner onto Genesee Street. "That would be simply awful."

"Look!" Tom tried to point with his big roll of bunting, and Abner stared. Big piles of lumber were scattered along the street, and men on ladders were building something.

"What are they doing?" Abner asked.

"They're building arches across the street,"

Tom said wisely. "When they're finished they'll be decorated with greens and streamers. Then General Lafayette will ride right through the arches when he rides down Genesee Street."

Abner was so interested in watching the carpenters that he was walking backwards.

"Abner!" cried Mrs. Scott sharply. "Turn around! The bunting will be in the dirt again if you don't watch out. Now hurry!"

Abner turned and trotted along behind Tom until they reached the Exchange Hotel. Here, too, there were men working on ladders all around the ballroom. The chandeliers had been decorated and the walls were being draped with red, white, and blue bunting and flowers and evergreens.

Tom and Abner stood holding their bundle of bunting while Mrs. Scott hurried off to the other end of the room. A workman approached them, but instead of taking the bundle he climbed up on a ladder beside them. A woman hurried past them with a large basket of flowers, but she paid no attention to them.

"Can't we put this down?" Abner whispered.

Tom looked for Mrs. Scott. "We'd better wait until someone tells us where to put it."

"I don't think anyone knows we're here," Abner said, looking around at all the people. "Where did Mrs. Scott go?"

Tom shook his head. "Maybe she went to find out where we should put this."

"My legs are getting tired," Abner said. "This stuff is scratchy, too."

"Boys!" Mrs. Scott called from the other end of the room. "Come here and put the bunting on this table."

Abner and Tom ran to place the bunting on the table, then turned to go.

"You boys go straight home now," Mrs. Scott called after them.

24

The boys ran down the steps and out the door to Genesee Street. Tom looked at Abner with a grin. "Come on!" he shouted. "Let's go!"

They started to run, but not toward home— only to the first of the arches. When they reached it, Abner had to tilt his head back to look up at the framework arching the street. Two men were fastening evergreen branches to the arch. One stood by a pile of branches on the ground and handed them up, one at a time, to a man on a ladder. This man threaded the branches through the framework, then fastened them in place with two or three nails.

The man on the ladder looked down at the boys. "Won't this be a sight for Lafayette to see when he comes tomorrow?" He smiled with pleasure. "All these arches standing in a row, all the way down Genesee Street, looking just as if they grew here!"

"Will General Lafayette's coach come right through this arch?" asked Tom.

"Indeed it will," the man answered. "Right down Genesee Street, through the middle of all these green arches with their flowers and red, white, and blue streamers. It ought to be a sight to see."

Shaking his head, the man on the ground said, "It's going to be a great day in Auburn—June 1st, 1825, the day General Lafayette visited Auburn, New York, all the way from Paris, France!" He handed up another branch to the man on the ladder. "It will be a real privilege to see a hero like him."

"Tom, what did General Lafayette do?" Abner asked without taking his eyes from the two men working on the arch.

The corners of Tom's mouth turned down in disgust. "Oh, Abner!" he exclaimed. "What did he do! You ought to know!"

Abner shook his head agreeably. "I know, but what *did* he do?"

"During the Revolutionary War General Lafayette came to America and helped the colonies win the war. That's what he did!" Tom took a deep breath and went on. "That was nearly fifty years ago, when he was young. Now he's visiting the United States again, and he's coming here to Auburn tomorrow."

"That's right, lad," said the man by the pile of branches, smiling and nodding his head. "Everybody is going to be here in Auburn—the Governor of New York, army officers, veterans of the Revolution. There'll be a big parade with a salute of big guns——"

Abner's brown eyes grew wide with excitement. "Guns?" he repeated.

"Yes, sir! A real twenty-four gun salute to the General! This will be a day you'll never forget, mark my words."

A Patriot's Name

"WELL, HELLO there! What are you two doing here?" Pa's voice boomed out behind the boys.

"Oh! Pa!" Pa's loud voice made Abner jump.

Tom laughed. "We helped Mrs. Scott bring some of the decorations down to the hotel."

Pa's face crinkled with a smile. "Shouldn't you be getting back home? Your mother will wonder where you are."

"Can't we go back to the newspaper office with you, Pa?" asked Abner.

"Not today, son. I have other things to do. There are many arrangements to be made for General Lafayette's visit."

"We'll get to see him, too, won't we?" Abner looked up at his father.

"Of course you will!" Pa laughed. "Everyone in Auburn will be here to see him." He looked across the street. "There's Judge Miller, and I want to talk with him. You boys go on home."

Tom jammed his hands into his pockets. "All right. Come on, Abner."

Abner took a deep breath. It seemed a shame to leave all the excitement. He walked along slowly beside Tom.

The trees swayed gently in the breeze. The lawns were green with new grass, and the air was fragrant with the perfumes of early summer flowers. The whole world had put on its prettiest clothing for today.

The boys walked along without speaking. They lingered here and there, scuffing their shoes in the dust. Abner looked up at the clear, bright sky. The sun looked as if it were standing still. He wondered whether today would ever end to make way for *the* day.

"Want to play ball?" asked Tom.

"Sure," Abner answered. "I'll get the ball." He started to run home.

"Wait. I bet Ma hasn't fixed it yet."

"Oh, I forgot about our ball." Abner's face was serious. Then he smiled. "Maybe she did."

"If she had time," said Tom.

"I wonder if she did have time." Abner shook his head. "Everybody is so busy!" He ran into the house, shouting, "Ma! Ma, did you mend our ball for us?"

Mother was sitting in the rocking chair by the window with her sewing in her hands. She didn't look up as she answered, "Over there."

Abner ran to the sideboard. He picked up the ball, which had been neatly sewn together again, and ran back to his mother. "Thanks, Ma!" He flung his arms around her neck.

30

"Abner! Be careful or you'll get stuck with my needle!" Ma said, but she was laughing at her son.

Abner ran out the door with the ball in his hand. "Tom! Tom! The ball is fixed!"

"Stand over there by the tree," Tom called as he ran toward the fence.

Abner went to the tree and when he turned saw Brownie coming slowly around the corner of the house. Brownie's head was down, but he was looking up at Abner with shining eyes and his tail wagged slowly and hopefully.

"Get ready!" Tom called. "Here it comes."

"Wait, Tom. Come look at Brownie."

Tom ran over to the tree and laughed when he saw Brownie. Both boys dropped to their knees and patted Brownie when he ran to them.

"You silly dog!" Abner said.

Brownie's tail wagged like a windmill and he panted happily.

Abner and Tom were both laughing when Ma came to the door. She smiled a little when she saw them, then called, "Abner. Tom. Put the dog up now so he won't get into any more trouble. Then both of you come here. There are many things for you to do."

Abner frowned, but he was really pleased. He was glad to be able to help as everyone else was doing.

"Boys, get the can of grease," Ma went on. "Tom you get the harness out of the barn and polish it. Abner, you get all the shoes and boots and polish them for tomorrow."

Abner lined the shoes and boots up on the kitchen floor. There were Ulysses' little boots with all their buttons, Amanda's slippers, Ma's slippers, Pa's big shiny black shoes, and the boots for Tom and himself. He sat cross-legged in front of the row and carefully covered each shoe with grease. Then, one by one, he rubbed and polished them with a soft cloth. When his nose began to itch he rubbed it with his sleeve, because he couldn't touch his face with his greasy, dirty hands.

Finally the shoes and boots all stood in a shiny, well-polished row. Abner got to his feet. He felt good that he had helped, but the work had made him hungry. He looked at the kitchen table. There was a loaf of freshly baked bread and a jar of jam on the table. He started to reach for the bread.

"Abner!" It was his mother's voice. "Don't touch that bread with your dirty hands!"

Abner looked at his hands. They did look a little dirty. "All right, Ma, but may I have some bread and jam if I wash them?"

"Well—only a small piece. It's almost suppertime." Ma looked at the row of shoes. "You did a good job with your polishing, Abner."

Suppertime finally came, and soon afterward

dusk fell. By now all preparations were finished. Candles were lighted and the children were sent to bed to dream of tomorrow.

The night was dark. Abner listened to the crickets and thought he would never go to sleep. Then suddenly he was awakened. The dark night was gone and sunlight poured through the window. He sat up quickly. He heard voices from the kitchen below—the low rumbling of his father's voice and the soft tones of his mother's replies.

Still in his nightshirt, he ran downstairs. The door was open and the hall was filled with sweet fresh summer air. He wriggled up his shoulders and shut his eyes as he breathed deeply. What a perfect day!

Suddenly a sharp noise cut the air. Abner jumped and ran into the kitchen. "Pa! What's that?" he cried.

Before his father could answer, there came another sharp report. Father smiled. "That is the beginning of the twenty-four gun salute to La-fayette. All the towns near us will hear it and come to the celebration."

Tom came running into the kitchen. "What was that noise? Did you hear it?"

Abner's eyes shone as he repeated his father's explanation. "We must hurry and get ready," he added. "We can't miss him!"

Like everybody else in Auburn, the Double-days dressed carefully in their Sunday clothes. Abner's tight white shirt collar was stiff and uncomfortable. He stretched his arms down as far as he could in his dark suit coat. It had been Tom's and was still a little large for Abner. Tom held his arms up because the sleeves of his coat were just a little short.

Ma stood straight in her good silk dress with a brooch at her throat and her good black shawl over her shoulders. Amanda looked very pretty in her new dress with the ruffles at the shoulders. Her soft brown hair was drawn back smoothly. Ulysses stood holding his sister's hand, his brown eyes shining in his freshly scrubbed face.

Ma looked proudly at her children. She straightened Tom's tie a bit and smoothed Abner's hair. Amanda giggled. As Ma's hand passed over Abner's hair a curl popped up. Ma laughed, too, and went to get a comb. She wet it in the water dripping from the pump and plastered Abner's hair down.

Abner shut his eyes and frowned. It was such a trial to have curly hair.

Ma stepped back and inspected the children again, then nodded her approval. "Let's go now."

THE PARADE

When the Doubledays reached Genesee Street it didn't even look like the street they knew. People were lined up on both sides of the street. The Doubledays joined the crowd and waited.

They waited a long time, it seemed to Abner. He looked down at his shiny boots and saw dust creeping over the toes. He stood on tiptoes and stretched his neck to look beyond the crowd. He put his hands in his pockets and waited.

Finally someone shouted, "Here he comes!"

Abner looked beyond the crowd again and saw a coach drawn by four big horses just coming into view. He took a deep breath and punched Tom with his elbow. "Look! Look!" People around him began to cheer.

The driver of the coach tightened his reins to slow the horses, and the coach rolled slowly along the street, passing under the green arches. Old soldiers along the street saluted and women and children waved.

General Lafayette took his hat from his head and waved to all the people along the way. Ab-

ner struggled to stay in front of the crowd, and Tom pushed forward beside him. General Lafayette nodded and smiled at them.

"Look, Tom!" Abner cried excitedly. "It's really Lafayette!"

In a moment the great man was past them. Abner and Tom ran into the street after the coach. They followed it as it rolled slowly to the open-air pavilion where the speeches were to be made.

At the pavilion Lafayette was met by the Governor of New York and other important men. They walked up the steps together to take their seats on the speaker's platform.

There were many speeches, and long ones. Abner's legs grew tired. It seemed as if everyone on the platform was going to make a speech. Abner tried to get his mother's attention. "Ma!"

She placed a finger on her lips. "Sh!"

"Ma, can we sit down, too?" He pointed to

Ulysses, who was sitting on the ground leaning against his mother's long skirts.

Ma leaned down to whisper, "It won't be much longer now."

"Will we go down to the hotel then?"

"Yes," Ma said. "Lafayette will be there."

People started to clap as one man finished speaking. Abner hoped this was the last speech, but in a few moments the crowd grew quiet and another man rose.

"Tom!" Abner whispered.

Tom didn't hear him. He was busy watching the big black horses that had drawn the General's coach. They were stamping their feet and rippling their shiny coats to make the flies move.

"Tom!" Abner nudged his brother with his elbow. "Where's Pa?"

"Up there." Tom pointed to a group of men at the back of the platform. "He's on the arrangements committee."

40

"The what?"

"The people who made all the plans for Lafayette to have a nice visit here," Tom explained.

"A nice visit! With all these speeches!"

Finally, however, the last speech was ended. General Lafayette climbed back into his coach and, followed by the crowd, rode to the ballroom at the Exchange Hotel.

THE NAME OF A PATRIOT

Amanda, Tom, and Abner were among the first to reach the hotel. They hurried upstairs to the ballroom and stood against a wall, waiting for their mother to arrive with Ulysses. She was breathless as she put Ulysses down and pulled her shawl in place and straightened her bonnet.

"Ma!" Abner said, tugging at her sleeve.

"Abner!" She frowned.

"But Ma, Pa wants us over there!"

Ma hadn't seen Pa beckoning to them from across the room. Now he came walking over to them. "Hester, come stand with me. I think the children may have a chance to meet him."

The family followed him and stood beside him near one end of the room. Soon the room was filled with people waiting for a closer glimpse of the General. They did not have long to wait. The door opened and the General's erect figure strode through it.

"Welcome, Lafayette!" everyone cried.

Slowly the General made his way around the room, stopping to shake hands with each person. By the time he reached Mr. Doubleday Abner was breathless with excitement.

Mr. Doubleday shook the General's hand and said, "My wife, sir——"

Lafayette bowed low over Mrs. Doubleday's hand. Mr. Doubleday put his arms around Amanda. "My daughter, Amanda——"

Amanda held the sides of her skirt and curtsied low. The General smiled and bowed.

Then Father motioned to the boys. "These are my three sons, Ulysses, Thomas, and Abner Doubleday."

The General took Ulysses' little hand briefly. He shook Tom's hand, then took Abner's hand in his large, firm grasp. "Abner? Abner Doubleday?" he asked.

Abner caught his breath. His cheeks grew red and his brown eyes opened wide as he murmured, "Yes, sir."

"Yes, General," Father said. "This is Abner Doubleday. He was named for his grandfather, Captain Abner Doubleday, who also fought in the Revolutionary War. Captain Doubleday was at Stony Point with General Anthony Wayne."

General Lafayette looked pleased. "You have a fine name, the name of a patriot," he told Abner. "May you also bring honor to the name."

Stony Point

Summer ended, and once again it was time for school. The woods and playing fields were quiet while the boys were at their desks. Games and fun came only at recess time and after school.

Each morning Abner carried his ragged leather ball to school to play ball during recess. All too soon, however, it was too cold to play ball. Winter winds blew down Genesee Street, and the few short hours the boys had to play outdoors were spent sliding down the hills and skating on the creek.

One evening in January, 1826, Abner and Tom were walking home from school, with their heads bent low against the cold north wind. The ground was covered with ice and swirling, powdery snow, and the path was slick.

Abner's dark eyes were shining and his cheeks were red with cold. "I'll beat you to the hitching post," he said.

"Try it!" Tom shouted. He ran a few steps, then slid on the dry, slick ice.

After a brief hesitation, Abner ran too, then threw himself forward to slide as fast and as far as he could. Suddenly his head and shoulders seemed to be going faster than his feet, and he felt himself falling. He tried to make his feet go faster, but they just went round and round in the air without getting him anywhere. He threw his hands forward to catch himself and his books flew in all directions.

"Oh! Oh, my!" he cried, and went sprawling across the ice.

Tom started to laugh and laughed until tears

rolled down his cold cheeks. "Abner, you looked just like a windmill going round," he said.

Abner grinned, a little disgustedly. Then he started to laugh, too. His books were all over the ground and his school bag had come open. The old leather ball rolled slowly on the snow.

Tom pointed to the ball. "What are you doing with that? You can't play ball in this kind of weather, Abner!"

Abner laughed again and shook his head. The ball did look funny. He scrambled to his feet and started to gather up his things.

Tom brushed him off and helped him pick up his books. "We'd better hurry home," he said. "It's getting dark."

Abner looked at the winter sky. It was dark and gray. Tom was right. It would be completely dark soon. "Let's run," he said.

"Not again!" Tom said. They laughed and Tom added, "We'd better hurry, though."

The wind was colder and stronger now. The dark branches of trees swayed stiffly before it. The boys lowered their heads and leaned into the wind as they walked on home.

They were glad to get home to a warm fire. The table was set for supper and Ulysses was playing in front of the kitchen fireplace.

"Put your books down, boys," Mother said. "Then go out and bring in some wood before you take off your coats."

"Oh, Ma!" Tom complained. "We're so cold!"

Ma smiled understandingly. "I know, but it will be easier now than later. We'll need the wood before the night is over."

Abner ran out to the woodpile with Tom close behind him. They each took as many big pieces of wood as they could carry and ran back to the house. Ma opened the door and they put their wood in the woodbox by the fireplace.

Abner took off his wraps, then stretched out

in front of the fire to get warm. Ma stood at the stove, shifting pots and pans here and there and stirring different kinds of foods, as she prepared supper. The kitchen smelled good with the warm, steamy odors of hot soup and freshly baked bread.

The faint, muffled sound of a dog barking reminded Abner that Brownie was missing. He got to his feet. "Where's Brownie?"

"In the barn," Ma answered. "I hear Pa coming in now. He'll bring Brownie in."

There was a loud slamming of doors and stamping of feet as Pa came into the kitchen.

Abner could hear Brownie jumping up and down and barking eagerly.

"My land!" Ma said as Pa entered the kitchen. "You sound like a whole army coming."

The house was warm and bright and filled with talk and laughter. It seemed good to Abner to have everyone inside on such a cold night.

"I have something for you, Hester," Pa said as he pulled a book from his coat pocket.

Ma looked over his shoulder. "Oh, good! *Phinney's Almanac.*"

Abner ran over to look. "What is an almanac?"

"It's a kind of calendar, son," Pa said, "but it's a lot more than that. It tells not only the months and the days, but the weather, holidays, and many other facts."

"I wouldn't know on which day to plant my garden if I didn't have the almanac to tell me," Ma said. "It tells when the moon will be full or half full, or not shining at all."

"The Phinney Publishing Company in Cooperstown publishes it every year," Pa added.

"I'm glad to have this one," Ma said. "Put it on the shelf by the stove."

"Just a minute, Hester," Pa said, smiling. "Look at the weather for the Fourth of July."

Ma wiped her hands on her apron and took the almanac. She leafed through the pages. "May, June—here it is—July Fourth——" Suddenly she exclaimed, "Snow!"

Tom came to look. "Snow? You mean that's the weather for the Fourth of July?"

"Oh, my! That just can't be!" Mother exclaimed. She shook her head. "The almanac is nearly always right, though."

Abner thought about the last Fourth of July. He remembered the ball game at the celebration and how hot he was. How could it ever snow on a hot July day?

Pa laughed. "The way it feels tonight, maybe it will never be warm again."

Abner wondered. It certainly was cold.

"Could this be?" asked Ma.

"I'm sure there is a mistake," Pa answered. "It's easy to make a mistake in a printer's office." Pa knew about such things because he published

the Auburn newspaper, the *Cayuga Patriot,*
every week.

After supper Tom and Abner carried in more
wood from the woodpile while Amanda helped
Ma with the dishes. Then the whole family sat
around the fireplace. Ma and Pa sat in their
rocking chairs, and the boys and Amanda sat on
the floor before the fire. Brownie curled up by
Abner and laid his head on Abner's knee.

The flames danced and the fire crackled with warmth. Abner's cheeks felt almost too hot. He stretched his feet out toward the fire.

"Be careful, Abner," Ma warned. "Don't get your boots too close to the fire. Before you get all settled, please go into the parlor and get my mending basket."

Abner looked at his mother. He didn't really want to go, but he knew he must. He got to his feet and walked toward the hall door.

"Take a candle so you can see," Pa said.

Abner picked up the candle holder and lighted the candle at the kitchen lamp. Then he walked into the cold hall. He cupped his hands around the candle flame so that it wouldn't go out. The parlor felt even colder and darker than the hall.

In the winter time the parlor was heated only when friends came to call. The furniture all looked stiff and the lace doilies cold and white.

He looked for the basket. As soon as he saw it on the candle table, he grabbed it and hurried back to the kitchen. It was nice to get back to the warm fire. The family looked cozy sitting there in the flickering light.

Abner gave the basket to Ma and sat down at her feet. Brownie looked up lazily, then came over to curl up beside Abner.

THE STORY OF STONY POINT

Abner looked up at Pa, who was contentedly watching the fire. Would Pa tell the story now? "Pa, what *did* Captain Abner Doubleday do during the Revolutionary War?"

Pa's eyes twinkled. Abner had asked the question many times since Lafayette's visit. Pa was glad that Abner was proud of his name and of the deeds of his grandfather.

"He fought at Bunker Hill, Abner."

Abner nodded. "Where else, Pa?"

"At Stony Point," Tom put in.

"With General 'Mad Anthony' Wayne?" Abner knew the answer already, but he asked the question anyhow. Then he put his elbows on his crossed legs and leaned forward, and Tom leaned forward, too. Pa's answer was the part they liked to hear.

Pa leaned back in his rocking chair and clasped his hands behind his head.

Abner smiled with anticipation. When Pa leaned back in his chair like that, the boys knew he was going to tell the story.

"Did Grandfather tell you the story when you were little, Pa?" asked Tom.

"Yes, he did," said Pa. "When I was a little boy I used to ask him to tell about the fighting for independence, just as you're asking now."

He looked up at the ceiling and narrowed his eyes a bit, then continued. "My father, Captain

Abner Doubleday, was one of seven brothers who served their country during the Revolutionary War. One of the brothers was Captain Seth Doubleday——"

"You mean our cousin Seth Doubleday in Cooperstown?" Amanda interrupted.

Pa smiled. "No, Amanda. This Captain Seth was the father of my cousin Seth in Cooperstown and the grandfather of your cousins there. Captain Abner fought in many battles during the Revolutionary War, but it was at Stony Point that he was captured and taken prisoner. He spent some time on the British prison ship 'Jersey.' After his release he joined the navy and served the rest of the war at sea."

Ma passed the basket of apples to Pa. Pa stopped his story and leaned forward to pick out a shiny red apple.

"Here, boys, have an apple," he said. Tom and Abner each took an apple.

"Hand me one, Abner," Amanda said.

Abner picked out two more apples and handed them to Amanda and Ulysses. Then they all sat eating their crunchy, juicy apples.

Abner watched Pa bite into his red apple. He waited for him to chew the bite and begin the story again. He waited and waited, but Pa just ate his apple, rocked in his chair, and looked into the blazing fire.

Finally Abner said, "Pa, would you finish telling about Stony Point?"

Pa laughed. "Abner, you know the story as well as I do. Why don't you tell it?"

Abner sat. He couldn't think of anything to say.

Father looked at the children's eager faces. "Oh, well—we'll tell it again." He drew a deep breath. "Let's see. Where were we?"

Abner grinned and sat up straight. "You were just going to tell about Stony Point."

"Stony Point was a huge rock fort in the Hudson River," Pa went on. "The colonists had held it first, but the British captured it. It was difficult to attack because of its rocky sides.

"The American troops were commanded by General 'Mad Anthony' Wayne, who led his men——"

"Why was he called 'Mad Anthony'?" Tom interrupted.

"He was called that because of his reckless courage," Pa said. "On July 15, 1779, General Wayne led his men fourteen miles over high mountains, through deep swamps and marshes, and along narrow roads. Most of the way was so difficult the men had to march single file."

"Did Grandfather march all that way, too?" asked Tom.

"He did. The soldiers' boots were soaked and their backs were tired from carrying their muskets, gunpowder, and lead all that way. They stopped to rest about a mile from Stony Point and made final plans. The men were to march in two columns side by side until they reached the fort. Each man was ordered to place a piece of white paper in his cap."

"Why, Pa?" asked Abner.

"The paper would help them to recognize one another in the dark and avoid being mistaken for the enemy," Pa explained. "General Wayne had planned the attack for a dark night so that the British would not see them coming."

He paused to take another bite of his apple, then went on. "After his men had fixed the papers in their caps, General Wayne gave them the password." His voice dropped to a whisper. " 'The fort's our own.' "

Tom and Abner leaned forward breathlessly. Abner felt tingly with excitement.

"Everything was still as the two lines moved forward," Pa continued. "When they came to the rock on which the fort was built, they separated. One line went to the right and the other to the left until the rock was surrounded."

Pa's voice grew louder. "General Wayne gave the signal, then with his sword in hand led his men up the sides of the cliff. When they reached the top they attacked the fort and retook it, shouting the password——"

"The fort's our own!"

Tom and Abner shouted the words at the tops of their voices. Mother laughed.

"My, what a noisy story!"

"Nevertheless, it was a very important victory, and Captain Abner Doubleday did his part in making it a victory," Pa said.

One Old Cat

ALTHOUGH it seemed that spring never would come, it finally did and the snow melted away. Abner and his friends were glad to be able to play ball again. Whenever three of them got together, they played ball. The weather grew warmer when summer came, and the prediction of *Phinney's Almanac* was nearly forgotten.

One June morning as the Doubledays were eating breakfast, Pa told the family that he had been chosen a member of the committee to plan the Fourth of July celebration.

"Oh, Pa, will the cannon be fired?" Abner wanted to know.

"I'm sure it will, Abner," Pa said, smiling. "I believe there will be a twenty-one gun salute at daybreak."

"Will there be a picnic?" asked Tom.

Pa nodded. "And speeches, too."

Abner and Tom looked at each other. "Do there have to be speeches, Pa?" Abner asked.

Pa's eyes twinkled. "Yes, Abner, there do have to be speeches. However, I expect there'll be ball games after the speeches."

So far Ma had just listened, but now she added with a sly smile, "Ulysses, don't forget the weather prediction in your planning."

"What?" Pa frowned, then laughed. "Oh, you mean snow?"

"Snow!" Tom cried. "On the Fourth of July?"

"Yes. Don't you remember the Almanac said there would be snow?"

Mr. Doubleday looked at his wife. "Surely you don't believe that, Hester?"

Mother's eyes looked merry. "It does seem unlikely," she said, "but that's what the Almanac says, Ulysses."

"It's only a printer's error," Pa said flatly. "Nothing more."

The conversation was interrupted by a call through the door. "Tom! Tom!"

Brownie leaped to his feet and ran to the door, barking. When he saw Charley at the door his tail started to wag.

Charley stuck his head in the door. "Want to play ball, Tom?"

"Sure, Charley," Tom said, getting up from the table. "Wait till I get my ball and bat."

"May I play, too?" asked Abner.

"Sure, come along," said Charley. "We'll play one old cat."

"Stay out of the mud, boys," Mother warned. Then she added, "And be back by lunch."

Pa smiled. Tom and Abner were making such

a clatter as they gathered up their things that he knew they didn't hear her.

The three boys ran down the path with Brownie chasing along behind them. Suddenly Brownie took a playful nip at Abner's heel.

Abner stopped. "Brownie, stop that!" Brownie's thick tail wagged happily.

As soon as Abner started to run again, Brownie took another nip at his boot. "Brownie, stop!" Abner commanded. "I've got to catch up with Tom and Charley."

Tom and Charley stopped in the broad field by the creek. Abner was breathless when he reached the field. "Can I catch first?" he panted.

Tom looked at Charley. Charley shrugged. "All right," he said. "I'll bat first then. Tom, you can throw."

Tom looked around for a tree to use as a goal. "All right," he said. He pointed to a tree thirty feet or so away. "That will be the goal. Abner, you stand here." He walked to a point about halfway between Abner and the tree but a little to one side. "I'll stand right here."

Charley picked up a flat rock and placed it on the ground in front of Abner. "This will be the hitter's rock."

BROWNIE WINS THE GAME

The boys put the extra bats in a pile. Tom took the ball and walked to the spot from which he would throw it to Charley. Charley took his bat, which was made from a flat board, and stood with his toe just touching the hitter's rock.

"Abner, stand back," he commanded as he raised his bat.

Abner moved back so that he wouldn't be hit by the bat when Charley swung at the ball. He watched Tom get ready to throw.

"Ready, Charley?" Tom yelled.

"Ready!" Charley answered.

Tom threw the ball underhand. Charley slammed it with his bat and started to run to the tree. Tom stepped backward, trying to keep his eye on the ball so he could catch it when it fell. It landed on a twig a couple of feet away, and rolled beyond his reach.

All the time Abner was yelling, "Get it, Tom! Get it!"

Charley reached the goal tree, tagged it, and turned back. He looked quickly at Tom and started back to the hitter's rock.

"Throw it here!" screamed Abner. "Throw it here!"

By the time Tom got the ball Charley was safe. "Count a tally for me!" he cried gleefully. "All right, Tom. Throw me another one."

Tom threw the ball again. Charley swatted the ball and started to run. This time Tom reached up and caught the ball in the air.

"Hooray!" shrieked Abner. Brownie ran from one boy to the other, barking and wagging his tail furiously. "My turn!" Abner yelled, picking up the bat.

Tom ran up and took the bat away from him. "It's my turn to bat," he said. "You throw and Charley will catch."

Abner frowned and walked out to the tosser's place. "All right," he said grudgingly. "Toss me the ball."

Tom threw him the ball, then crouched over the hitter's rock, bat ready. Abner threw the ball and Tom swung and missed. Charley threw the ball back to Abner.

Again Abner threw and again Tom swung his bat. This time the ball flew over Abner's head. Abner ran to get it and turned back just as Tom touched the tree. Abner threw quickly. Charley caught the ball with outstretched hands and tagged Tom before he reached the hitter's rock.

"No tally for Tom!" he cried. "Come on, Abner, now it's your turn."

With a grin Abner started toward the hitter's rock. At that moment his friend Hans walked up.

"Hi there, Abner. Can I play, too?"

"Not now, Hans," Charley said.

Hans looked disappointed. Abner felt sorry for him. "Let him play, Charley," he said. "We can use another player."

"No, go on," Hans said as he leaned against a tree. "I'll just watch."

"Come on, Abner, get the bat!" Tom yelled.

Abner picked up the bat and held it out in front of him, ready and waiting. Charley threw the ball. Abner leaned forward and swung at it as hard as he could. There was a thud and the ball soared high.

Abner started to run. Out of the corner of his eye he could see the ball still in the air and Charley running to catch it.

Suddenly Abner tripped and almost fell. Something was pulling at his boot. He pulled himself away and tried to run on, but there was a yank at the other heel. He stumbled again, caught himself, and struggled on. With each step there was a nip at his heel.

He looked down and saw Brownie. "No, Brownie, no!" he cried desperately. "Stop it!"

By this time Charley had picked up the ball and was running toward him.

"Let go, Brownie!" Abner screamed. "I have to run!"

Tom sank to the ground, weak with laughter.

"You'll have to leave Brownie home if you want to make a tally, Abner," Hans shouted.

Charley was laughing, too, as he ran up and tagged Abner with the ball. "Brownie put you out, Abner," he said.

Abner was disgusted. He would have made a tally if it hadn't been for Brownie. He looked down at Brownie, who seemed to be laughing, then sank to the ground with a sigh. Brownie sat beside him and looked up into his face. When Abner ignored the dog, he pushed his nose gently under Abner's arm until it was completely around his neck.

Abner smiled sadly. He couldn't stay mad at Brownie long. "All right, Brownie," he said. "You won the ball game—just because you won't let me run!"

THE FOURTH OF JULY

The plans for an exciting celebration of Independence Day were complete. There would be church in the morning, a picnic dinner at noon, and ball games for the boys in the afternoon. Abner and Tom decided that Brownie would have to stay home. "He has won enough ball games for the other boys," Abner declared.

The twenty-one gun salute awakened Abner at daybreak. The sky was dark and gray. By the time the church bells rang to celebrate the country's birthday the sun was shining, but it was silvery and pale.

It was a chilly morning. The children wore jackets and Mother pulled a heavy shawl around her shoulders. "Do you think it's cold enough for snow?" she asked Pa teasingly.

Pa smiled. "It is uncommonly chilly, Hester, but I don't think it will snow just to oblige a printer's mistake."

Father, Mother, Tom, Abner, Amanda, and Ulysses went to church for the Independence Day services. There were prayers and the choir sang. Then the minister, Mr. Bostwick, read the Declaration of Independence. Abner sat quietly, listening, but he was glad when the service was over and he could go outside.

Everyone walked in a big parade to the picnic

grounds. The long tables were already set up and in a short time were laden with all the good food the ladies of the town had prepared.

Abner thought the day was strange for the Fourth of July. The pale sun had disappeared and the sky was cloudy and gray again. As he heard the ladies talk about the weather, he shivered and turned his coat collar up around his neck. Then he looked up at the sky. For a moment he couldn't believe his eyes.

"Ma! Ma, look!" he cried at last, pointing to the tiny snowflakes that were floating down from the clouds. "Ma, it's snowing!"

"Where?" asked Pa in disbelief. Then, he, too, saw the fluttering snowflakes.

"Phinney's Almanac was right!" Ma exclaimed.

Everyone began to talk and laugh at once. Snow—snow on the Fourth of July!

The Woods behind Fort Hill

Autumn was beautiful that year, golden and warm. Though Brownie had been shut out of the ball games, he went to school with Abner and Tom every day. While they were studying inside, he lay by the door, waiting for them.

At recess, when the schoolyard was filled with happy laughing children, Brownie ran and played with them. When they were called inside again, he took up his place by the door and waited for school to be out.

Today his head lifted when he heard the scufing of feet that told him school was over for the day. He jumped up and waited with wagging tail, watching for the boys. Finally Abner ran out the door and down the steps, swinging his books in their leather strap at his side.

"Hi, Brownie," he called. Brownie came running up and Abner rubbed his head. "Would you like to go to the woods?"

Brownie barked and wagged his tail.

Charley ran up to Abner. "You going to the woods?" he asked.

"Yes," Abner answered. "Come along."

"All right. What will we do with our books?"

"We can take them along." Abner threw his book strap over his shoulder and started to run. "Come on!"

"Abner!"

Abner turned to see Hans running after him. "What are you going to do?"

"We're going up to the woods to explore," he said. "Come on!"

The three boys and the dog ran down the narrow board walk until they came to a field, then ran through the field to the woods.

Abner loved to walk through the woods. Golden sunlight came through the trees in narrow bands of light. The trees were tall and dark, and their leaves formed a roof overhead. The path was muddy and covered with old leaves.

"Let's leave our books here on this log," Abner suggested. He pointed to a huge gray trunk lying beside the path.

Charley put his load of books down, but Hans hesitated. "Are you sure they'll be all right? My father would wallop me good if I lost my books," he said.

"Of course they'll be all right," Abner said, disgusted. "What could happen to them?"

"Someone might take them," he said.

"Who would want them?" Charley asked.

"We might not be able to find them again," Hans added doubtfully.

Abner laughed. "Oh, we'll not get lost in this woods! I'll make a map."

He pulled a piece of paper from his pocket. With a lead pencil, he drew the log and marked it with an X. "Here it is, Hans." He put the paper in his pocket. "Now let's be army scouts looking for Indians."

"All right," Charley agreed eagerly. "You be the leader."

Abner walked carefully and quietly ahead. "Don't make too much noise—and watch!"

"Watch behind every tree," Charley whispered to Hans. "There may be Indians hiding."

The three boys crept along, looking from side to side. Abner walked a little ahead. Once he climbed a small hill. When Charley and Hans reached the top of the hill and started down the other side, Abner had disappeared.

Charley and Hans looked at each other. Hans opened his mouth to call, but Charley raised one hand. "Shh! We might be heard!" He crouched low and looked carefully on either side of the path. Then he saw Abner and Brownie through the shrubbery.

"This way," Abner said softly as he marked their place on his map.

A SHADOW IN THE WOODS

The boys followed Abner through the forest. Here the trees grew so close together that the sky was almost hidden. The boys stepped over logs and walked on the trunks of fallen trees.

Suddenly Hans cried, "Oh, look!"

"Sh-h-h!" Charley and Abner said, then added in a whisper, "What is it?"

Hans pointed to a big tree ahead of them. Lurking behind it was a shadow!

The boys crouched and huddled together, Hans behind Abner.

"What could it be?" whispered Charley.

"Maybe it *is* an Indian," Hans said fearfully.

"Wait here," said Abner. "Let me see." He flattened out on his stomach and crawled slowly through the underbrush with Brownie at his side. He circled to the right of the tree and tried to keep Brownie flat beside him.

It seemed to take him hours to crawl the few feet to a point where he could see behind the tree. Then suddenly he stood up and laughed.

"What is it?" called Hans and Charley.

"Come see." Abner pointed. "It's just a log propped up against the tree."

"It certainly made a shadow that looked like a man," Charley said.

"The forest is full of shadows now," said Hans in a worried tone.

The boys looked about them. The woods were growing darker and darker, and gloomy shadows were everywhere.

"Let's go!" cried Charley.

"Yes, let's," agreed Hans, "but which way?"

The forest seemed to have closed in around them. There was no path here and the boys had turned around when they were looking for the shadow behind the tree. Now they didn't know which way to go.

Abner took out his map. "We go to a big rock and then we turn. Let's see—going back, we would turn to the right."

They looked around but could see no rock. "You stand here," said Abner. "I'll walk this way for a short distance to see if I can find it."

He walked away, calling back from time to time. Although he went farther and farther, he found no rock. At last he returned. "All right, Hans. You walk the other way and we'll wait."

Hans walked away slowly, with Brownie running ahead of him. Suddenly he shouted with relief, "Here it is, Abner! Here it is!"

Abner and Charley ran to join Hans. They all laughed and Abner said, "I know how we go now. We walk just a little way till we come to an enormous tree across the path."

In a few minutes, following the landmarks on Abner's map, the boys found their way back to the log on which they had left their books. They picked their books up and ran out of the woods, with Brownie running ahead of them.

"We're really late!" Charley exclaimed. "See how dark it is everywhere."

"We'd better hurry," said Hans.

The three boys began to run.

The moment Abner closed the kitchen door behind him, he could hear his mother's voice. "Abner, where *have* you been?"

He stood by the door with muddy hands and face. His shirt and waistcoat were covered with brown leaves and mud. His face was scratched from the underbrush.

Mother frowned. "Are you hurt, Abner?"

"No, Ma." Abner frowned, too. He really hadn't known he was going to be so late.

Just then Pa walked in the door. "Am I still in time for supper?"

"Yes, Abner just got home. Look at him!"

"Well, son, what's this?" Pa's dark eyes looked directly into Abner's face.

"I'm sorry I'm late, Pa—and muddy. We were playing in the woods and didn't know the time."

"All right, son. Go wash up for supper."

Mother looked after Abner. "Do you think it's safe for Abner to play in the woods?"

"Oh, I think so, Hester. Boys have to be able to play in the woods."

Mother shook her head. "I suppose so, but it seems to me Abner is either muddy from the woods or muddy from playing ball."

Mr. Doubleday laughed. "That's the way it is with boys!"

A Ride on the Stagecoach

"THROW IT here, Charley!" Abner shouted.

Charley turned and threw the ball to Abner's outstretched hands. Abner wheeled and threw it at John. It hit him on the shoulder just as he reached for the fence post.

"You're out, John!" shouted Hans.

John put a hand to his shoulder and frowned as he walked away from the fence. "Just you wait, Abner Doubleday! I'll get you good!"

Abner laughed. "All right, try! Here's your chance. It's my turn to bat." He picked up the bat and took his place at the batter's stone. Hans got ready to throw the ball.

John still looked angry. He watched carefully as Hans threw the ball and Abner hit it. Then as it soared overhead he ran to catch it.

Abner didn't look to see where the ball went— he just ran as fast as he could. John picked it up quickly and threw it at Abner with all his might.

"Watch it, Abner!" Charley shouted.

Throwing himself to the ground, Abner slid toward the tally post.

"You made it!" Charley shouted gleefully. "You made it!"

Suddenly John whirled and ran toward Charley with his fists up. His eyes were black with anger. "He made it because you helped him!"

Hans ran for the ball, which was still rolling slowly over the ground, and Abner picked himself up and brushed the dust from his pants.

The school bell rang, signalling the end of recess. John dropped his fists slowly. "Just you wait till lunch time," he warned. Then he turned and stomped off.

There was no ball game at lunch time, however. Mr. Hansen, the teacher, took one look at the dirty boys and made them stay in.

After eating, Abner worked at his Latin. With his head resting on his hand, he worked slowly and carefully, writing his English translation on his slate.

He was sitting near the big fireplace that heated the one-room building. Mr. Hansen still kept a fire going even though it was April, and as he worked Abner began to grow hot. Beads of perspiration stood out on his lip and he wiped his face on his sleeve.

Pausing, Abner looked out the open window across the room at the soft blue sky. He wished he sat by the window where he could smell the fresh spring air. Then he smiled. In only two weeks school would be over and he would be free for the rest of the summer. He could hardly wait for those two weeks to end.

"Abner." Mr. Hansen's voice broke into his thoughts. "Have you finished your Latin?"

"Yes, sir." Abner stood beside his seat as he answered.

Mr. Hansen smiled. He had known this would be the answer. He could always depend on Abner to finish his work promptly and well. Abner was one of his best pupils.

"HERE COMES THE STAGE!"

Finally the long school day was over. Abner ran down the steps and out into the wonderful warm spring day. Charley soon caught up with him and they ran along the walk together. Abner breathed deeply. The fresh air smelled good.

"Look, Abner," Charley cried. "Here comes the stage down Genesee Street!"

86

Abner looked at the swaying coach. Four huge sweating horses were pulling it.

"It's coming mighty fast, Abner," Charley said. "Do you think——"

Abner grinned. He knew what Charley was going to say. "Sure, let's hitch a ride," he said. "We can make it."

Just then the pounding horses passed in front of them and the two boys ran out and grabbed the trunk rack on the back of the stage. Abner

was panting, but he reached down to grasp Charley's arm and help him up on the rack.

Once perched safely on the rack, the boys grinned at each other. Their faces were red with excitement. The stage rocked and bounced as it rolled swiftly over the rough street. Dust rolling up from the rear wheels engulfed them.

Suddenly the air was filled with the shrill blast of a horn. Abner laughed.

"It's Jim Burgess!"

Charley nodded in agreement. Jim Burgess was the driver perched on the driver's box at the front of the coach. He always blew on his horn as he came into town.

The horses slowed to a walk and the brakes squealed as Burgess tightened them against the wheels. The coach rolled slowly to a stop in front of the Exchange Hotel.

Abner and Charley jumped from the rack as quickly as they could and ran to the board walk.

They were not quick enough, however. Jim Burgess saw them and shouted, "Hey, you there! You know you're not supposed to hitch rides!" His tough leathery face was stern.

Abner and Charley bent their heads sheepishly. Abner kicked at the dirt between the boards of the sidewalk.

Jim walked over to them and placed a big hand on the dusty head of each. "All right, lads," he said in a kindly voice. "I won't say anything to your fathers this time, but don't do that again. It's dangerous and you might get hurt."

Abner and Charley nodded and ran off. They knew they didn't have to be afraid of Jim Burgess. He was always good to the boys in town.

They were still breathing a little hard from the excitement of the ride. They stood in front of the hotel and watched the passengers climb down from the stagecoach. Milton and John Sherwood, who owned the stagecoach line, came out to greet the travelers and to help unload their baggage and carry it into the hotel.

Abner always enjoyed watching the stagecoach come into town. He liked to look at the horses and the big coaches. He liked to listen to the passengers' conversation. Above all, he found it exciting to think of all the faraway places a stagecoach could take you.

A Robber

It was the day after school was out that Charley, Hans, and Abner had their exciting adventure. It had seemed to them that school would never end, but finally the last day came, and with it the day of the school picnic. Abner could hardly believe it.

When the picnic lunch was over the boys started to play ball on the school ground. They whooped and yelled with delight, happy to know that a whole summer lay before them—a summer with nothing to do but play ball, explore the forest, watch stagecoaches, and fish and swim in the creek near the school.

They tossed their caps and books anywhere. They laughed and screamed and ran. They all made tallies in the ball game, and even John wasn't angry at anyone.

At last Mr. Hansen said, "All right, boys, you may go whenever you wish. School is over until next fall."

Abner and Charley whooped together, "Hooray for Mr. Hansen!" Then they gathered up their belongings and ran down the street.

As they ran along Abner said, "Why don't we watch the stages come in?"

"That's a good idea," Charley said.

Hans, John, and the other boys agreed, so they all walked down to the Exchange Hotel. When they reached the stage office next door to the hotel they were hot and tired. They threw down their books and leaned against the veranda of the hotel to wait. They waited and watched all afternoon, but no stagecoach arrived.

One by one the boys grew tired and went home. Finally Charley said, "Abner, I think I'd better go. It must be nearly suppertime, and I'm getting hungry."

Abner looked down the long street toward the edge of town, but there was no coach in sight. "I guess we might as well go," he said. He picked up his books and the two boys started to walk slowly homeward. Abner was disappointed. "Maybe we could see the early stage tomorrow morning," he said.

"Sure we could," Charley agreed. "I'll meet you here early in the morning."

That was how the great adventure began.

THE ROBBERY

Early the next morning Abner looked out the window of his room. The sun wasn't up yet, or if it was, it was hidden by clouds. He listened quietly. He could hear the voices of his father and mother in the kitchen.

A feeling of excitement went through him as he realized he didn't have to go to school. He looked out the window again. It was misty outdoors, but the moist air was warm. He had a feeling this was going to be an exciting, adventure-filled day.

"Where are you going in such a hurry?" his mother asked as he rushed through breakfast.

"I'm going to meet Charley. We're going to watch the stagecoaches," he answered between bites. "May I be excused now?"

The expression on Ma's face didn't change, but her eyes had a merry look. "Abner, you have all summer. You don't need to hurry so."

"But Ma, there's so much to do."

Mrs. Doubleday laughed. "All right, on your way then. Hurry!"

Abner ran out the door and down the path.

Brownie jumped up and ran after him, and together they hurried to the Exchange Hotel. Charley and Hans were already there, waiting.

"Hey, Charley! Hans!" Abner called as he hurried up.

The two boys ran to meet him. "Abner! Abner! Wait till you hear!" they cried excitedly.

"Hear what?" he asked. He couldn't imagine what their excitement was about.

"The stage was robbed last night!" Charley shouted.

Abner stopped short. "Robbed? What do you mean, Charley?"

"A robber held up the stage last night and took a trunk from it," Hans explained.

Abner couldn't believe it. "Who would want to do that?" he said.

Charley shrugged. "No one knows." Then he added, "Let's look in the stage office. Maybe we can find out something more."

The boys ran up on the hotel veranda and leaned against the window to peer inside. Mr. Milton Sherwood, one of the owners of the stage line, was talking with three men. They all seemed excited. A woman was sitting on a chair in one corner of the office, holding a handkerchief to her face. She looked pale and frightened.

The boys stepped back and looked at one another. "You mean they didn't catch the robber?" Abner said. His eyes were large and round as he thought for a moment. "Was it the stage Jim Burgess drives?"

Hans shook his head. "No, it was the stage that comes in early in the morning."

"Let's go inside," Abner said. "Maybe we can hear what they're saying."

The three boys slid in through the open door. There was so much excitement inside the grown-ups didn't even know they were there.

Now the boys could see that the woman was

close to tears. "Oh, dear! Oh, dear!" she murmured. "I scarcely know what to do!" She put
her handkerchief to her mouth, then added, "All
our clothes were in that trunk."

"The trunk must have belonged to her," Abner
whispered to Charley.

Milton Sherwood's face was troubled. He bent
over the woman and said, in a sympathetic voice,
"Madam, it would be best for you to go to your
hotel room and rest. We will do our best to find
your trunk for you."

The boys slipped back outside. The mist was
beginning to disappear now, but the day was
still quite gray.

Abner frowned. "Where could Mr. Sherwood
look to find her trunk?"

Hans shook his head. "I don't know."

"You wouldn't think anyone would steal a
trunk right here in Auburn," Abner said with a
serious expression. "And why did they take the

trunk? She said the trunk contained all their clothes, but she didn't mention anything else."

"Maybe the person who took it thought it contained money or something," Charley said. "Anyhow, what shall we do now? There won't be another stage for two hours."

Abner looked up and down the street. Nothing was stirring. The village was quiet. "Why don't we go to the woods?" he suggested.

"It might rain," Charley said doubtfully, looking at the gray sky.

"Even if it does, the weather's warm," Abner said. "We wouldn't get very wet in the woods. The trees would protect us."

"But it's easy to get lost if the sun isn't shining," said Charley.

"Oh, don't worry about that," Abner replied. "I can make a map as we go along." He started running toward the woods, with Brownie at his heels, and the others followed reluctantly.

The huge trees stood straight and tall against the gray sky, their green leaves stirring slightly in the still air. The boys followed a path that led into the darkness of the forest. The land was hilly here, and the path rose and fell with the hills. Brownie ran ahead, waiting from time to time until the boys caught up with him.

Finally Charley stopped. "Wait up, Abner!" he called and sank down on a log to rest.

Abner looked around. It was almost dark here. The branches and leaves overhead shut out the pale light of day.

Charley shivered a little. The forest seemed to close in on them, gloomy and dark, and there wasn't a sound. "It's scary, isn't it?" he whispered.

Hans nodded slowly and glanced anxiously from side to side. "It's so dark!" he replied in a hushed voice.

Abner came back to sit beside his friends. "It is, a little," he said. His eyes were wide, too, and he looked about cautiously. Above him, the leaves of the trees were dark and shiny, and he could smell the early summer freshness of the air. Near by a few pale flowers were pushing their way through last year's dead leaves.

Suddenly there was a slight crackling noise. Charley grabbed Abner's sleeve and Hans whispered, "What was that?" in a frightened voice.

Abner looked about slowly. "I don't know," he said. "Maybe it was a squirrel or a chipmunk."

Then they heard the noise again, more distinctly—a kind of scraping sound. Charley sat up straight. He didn't move his head but moved his eyes from far right to far left.

Abner stiffened and listened, too. The sound seemed to come from above. He looked up and saw a man sitting on a branch in a near-by tree, half hidden by leaves.

"Hans! Charley!" he whispered, punching the others. "Look!"

Charley's eyes followed Abner's gaze. "Oh! Let's get out of here!" he cried, and started to run.

Abner and Hans ran, too. Brownie began to bark, but when the boys ran he also ran. They all ran as fast as they could, deeper and deeper into the forest.

At last Abner halted. "We're far enough now," he said, panting. "Let's stop."

"Did you see him?" Charley asked. "He was all shabby and—and——"

"He looked mean!" blurted Hans.

"Yes, he did look mean," said Abner. He hesitated a moment, thinking. "Do you suppose—could he be the robber?"

"The robber?" Hans gave a little whistle. "Do you reckon?"

The boys walked on, slowly and thoughtfully.

The Lost Trunk

"WHAT ARE we going to do?" Charley said. He sounded frightened.

Abner wasn't listening. He had left the path suddenly and was forcing his way through the underbrush. His face was serious and intent.

"Where are you going?" asked Hans.

"Look!" Abner pointed to a dark object almost hidden by brambles.

"Wait, Abner!" Charley cried. "Let's stay together." He and Hans hurried to catch up with Abner.

By this time Abner had reached the object. "Charley! Hans! Look! It's the trunk!"

Charley and Hans hurried to Abner's side. He was looking down at a large black trunk that had been pushed under the bushes.

"That's the trunk the lady was talking about," Hans said.

"Look, here's the rope. The thief must have dragged the trunk here through the brambles," Abner said. He leaned down and picked up a piece of rope beside the trunk.

"Well!" Charley leaned against the trunk in amazement, while Hans bent down to inspect the trunk closely.

"The lock has been broken," Hans said.

Abner looked at the lock. "I wonder if the robber took anything out?"

"Maybe there's gold in it, and treasures and things like that," Charley said hopefully.

"Let's open it and see," suggested Hans.

The boys swung the heavy rounded lid of the trunk open and their faces fell. There was no treasure inside, only a tangled mass of clothing. Someone had mussed the clothing up searching for something, and the trunk was only about half full.

"Maybe the robber took all the gold and just left these clothes," Charley suggested.

Abner frowned. "We ought to get this trunk back to the hotel."

"But how, Abner?" Charley pushed on the side of the trunk. "I can't even budge it."

"Maybe we can if we all work together," Abner said. "Here, Hans, let's put this rope around it." Abner picked up the rope and added, "Charley, help me lift the trunk up so Hans can slip the rope underneath."

Together the boys pushed and tugged until Hans was able to slip the rope under the trunk.

"Now let's make a hard knot," Abner instructed. "Then put the rope under the trunk again and tie it the other way."

They worked and worked until they finally got the rope around the trunk and tied securely. They left a short piece of the rope at one end with which to pull the trunk.

When they had finished Abner wiped his forehead with the back of his hand. His hair was curling from the warmth of the work and from the dampness of the day. Impatiently he shoved his hair back with his hand.

Charley and Abner got in front of the trunk and Hans in back. Abner put the end of the rope over his right shoulder and Charley took hold of it just behind him. Hans leaned on the trunk, ready to shove.

Abner looked over his shoulder at Hans and then at Charley. "Ready, Hans?"

Hans nodded.

"All right, Charley, now *pull!*" He and Charley pulled with all their might and Hans shoved. They tugged and they pushed, but the heavy trunk had settled into the soft earth and would not move. Finally the boys stopped.

Abner straightened himself with a deep sigh and leaned against a tree. "I don't think we can do it," he said.

"If we can't even move it, how do you suppose the robber got it here?" asked Hans.

"Maybe there were two men," Abner said.

All three of the boys were breathing deeply, trying to regain their breath.

"That may be," said Charley with lifted eyebrows, "but if so, where is the other robber?"

Abner's eyes twinkled with mischief. "Maybe he's right behind you."

Charley jumped and looked over his shoulder. Hans and Abner both laughed.

"I don't think that's funny," Charley said.

Abner picked up the rope again. "Let's try once more," he said.

Still looking glum, Charley got behind Abner

and they both tugged with all their might while
Hans shoved from behind. The trunk moved,
but only a few inches. They rested a moment,
then tried again, but still without success.

Abner sank down on the ground right where he was. Hans leaned against a tree, and Charley sat beside Abner with his elbows on his knees and his chin in his hands.

Abner frowned thoughtfully. The ground under him was damp and the forest seemed dark and unfriendly.

"I guess we'll just have to walk back to town and tell Mr. Sherwood where the trunk is," he said at last.

"What if we can't find our way back again?" asked Hans.

"What if the robbers should come back for it when we leave?" asked Charley.

Abner was silent for a moment. "I know, Charley. You go back to town and tell Mr. Sherwood where the trunk is. Hans and I will stay here to guard it."

"Me!" cried Charley. "I don't think I can find my way. Besides, what if I see the robbers?"

"I'll make a map for you," said Abner. "You can find your way out of the woods and then you'll have a map to guide you back here to the trunk."

Abner took out his piece of paper and with a stub of pencil started to sketch the map quickly. He knelt beside the trunk and used its top for a desk.

"You don't need to go in the way we came," he said. "You can take the other fork of the path, which will be closer to town anyway." He worked hastily. "Here, I'll show you."

"But what if I see the robbers?" Charley interrupted. "What if they try to stop me?"

Abner looked at Charley's frightened face. "All right, Hans, you go with Charley and I'll stay here. Hans, you look at the map, too."

Charley and Hans both leaned over the trunk to see the map.

110

"You go this way to the crooked oak tree," Abner explained, "and then you turn north——"

"Which is north?" asked Charley.

Abner looked at his friend with disgust. "This way on the map," he said and put an arrow and a big N on the map. "Your right side as you walk," he added, then paused a moment. "But you'd better run—just in case!"

Hans looked troubled. "But Abner, if I go with Charley, what about you? I don't think we ought to leave you all alone. What if the robbers come back here?"

Abner straightened his back and held his chin up stiffly. "I'll be all right. Besides, I won't be alone. Brownie will be with me. Now you two hurry to town!"

The Map

ABNER SWALLOWED hard as he watched his friends walk down the path. They walked slowly for a while, then started to run.

Abner slid down to sit with his back propped against the trunk and put his arms around Brownie. Brownie seemed fat and solid under his thick brown fur. When he panted his breath was warm and moist against Abner's face.

The two of them watched until Hans and Charley disappeared beyond the first small hill. Then Abner took a deep breath and looked about slowly. The shadows were deep, and though he strained his eyes he could see little

112

but shadows and the vague trunks and lower branches of near-by trees. He could hear the faint sounds of the forest—birds chirping and scolding in the trees, forest animals moving softly and stealthily through the shadows.

He felt snug and safe sitting close to the trunk with Brownie curled up beside him, watching his face. Suddenly Brownie lifted his head and growled softly deep in his throat. Abner sat up straight, his heart pounding.

"What is it, boy?" he whispered.

The hair on the back of Brownie's neck bristled and he got to his feet. Abner held him with one arm around his neck and looked about fearfully, half afraid of what he might see.

Suddenly a rabbit came bounding out of the underbrush. Brownie grew tense.

Abner snorted. "Brownie! You dog! Sit down!" He smiled, but at the same time he was relieved to know it was only a rabbit that had found them. "You behave, Brownie. We haven't any time for rabbit chasing now."

Brownie turned to listen to Abner, then sat down again and laid his head on Abner's knee.

OUT OF THE WOODS

Charley and Hans ran so fast they didn't stop to look at the woods around them. From time to time they slowed down a little to look at the jiggling map which Charley clutched in his hands, but they didn't stop. When they decided which way to go, they ran faster than ever. They didn't stop running until they were out of the woods.

When they reached town, Charley shoved the map in his shirt pocket and they hurried along the board walk to the hotel and the stage office. Neither of them spoke, and they walked as fast as they could. Hans thought of Abner waiting alone in the woods and frowned. "Come on! Hurry!" He grabbed Charley's arm.

Charley jerked his arm loose. "What do you mean, hurry? I *am* hurrying!"

They pushed through the door at the stage coach office. Several men were inside, talking earnestly. They looked up when the two boys, red-faced and excited, burst through the door.

"Mr. Sherwood!" Charley shouted.

Milton Sherwood rose from his desk. "What is it, boy?"

"We found the—we saw the robber——" Charley talked fast.

"Wait a minute," Mr. Sherwood said.

"Oh, sir, we found the trunk in the woods!" Hans interrupted.

At that moment Abner's father walked through the door from the hotel lobby.

"Oh, Mr. Doubleday," Charley cried breathlessly, "Abner may be in trouble!"

Mr. Doubleday frowned. "What do you mean, Charley? What is all this?"

Milton Sherwood turned to Mr. Doubleday. "The boys are so excited we don't know the whole story, but they've apparently found the stolen trunk in the woods."

"Yes, sir," said Hans, "and Abner's staying with it until we get back!"

"Abner?" Mr. Doubleday was very serious. "Where is he, Hans?"

"We have a map." Charley pulled the map from his pocket and handed it to Mr. Doubleday.

"Did Abner make this map, Charley?" Mr. Doubleday asked, glancing at it.

"Yes, sir."

"Did you say you saw the robber?" Milton Sherwood asked.

"Yes, sir, up in a tree, and then we ran," Hans said. "We ran on into the woods, and then we found the trunk."

Mr. Doubleday and Mr. Sherwood looked at each other. "Let's go!" said Mr. Doubleday and started out the door.

"Come on!" Mr. Sherwood said to the other men in the office and ran after Mr. Doubleday.

Charley and Hans led the way back to the woods, and the men followed. Charley led them into the woods, but when he came to a fork in the path he stopped and scratched his head uncertainly. A patch of pale sunlight lay on the brown leaves in the path ahead of him.

"What's wrong, Charley?" Mr. Doubleday demanded impatiently.

"I'm not sure which way to go," Charley said.

"Let me see your map." Mr. Doubleday looked at the map quickly. "We take the left fork here. Come on!"

The forest was still except for the crackling of twigs under their feet. Mr. Sherwood turned to Hans. "Where did you see the man?"

"A little way down this path," Hans said. He lowered his voice and looked up. "He was up in a tree."

Without slowing down, Mr. Doubleday looked into the tree overhead. "He's not likely to still be here."

"Where's Abner?" Mr. Sherwood demanded.

"It won't be much farther now," said Charley.

"Well, let's hurry," said Mr. Sherwood.

By this time they were all running. "The trunk is right over there," Hans said, pointing to the thicket.

"Hallo! Abner!" shouted Mr. Doubleday.

Abner's voice sounded thin and far away as he answered, "Over here, Pa!"

A REWARD

Abner took a deep breath. His father's voice sounded good. He stood up. It seemed a long time since Charley and Hans had gone for help. He had watched carefully all about him but had seen nothing but shadows and Brownie's rabbit. It was a welcome sight to see his father coming through the thicket with Charley and Hans and a whole crowd of men behind him.

"Abner!" Pa cried. "Are you all right?"

Abner stood straight and tall beside the trunk. A wide grin lighted his face. "I'm all right, Pa," he said.

Mr. Doubleday put his big strong arm around Abner's shoulder. Milton Sherwood smiled at Abner and said, "You're a reliable guard."

Brownie ran around in circles, barking delightedly at all the excitement.

"There's the trunk, all right," said Mr. Sherwood. "Mrs. Taylor will be very pleased to get it back."

"Is anything left in it?" someone asked.

Charley ran over to open it. "I think some of

the things must be gone, but it's still about half full," he said.

Mr. Sherwood looked in. "I guess the thief took everything of value, but at least there are some clothes here."

"The boys already have the rope around the trunk," Mr. Doubleday said. "Let's try to get it back to town."

The four men gathered around the trunk and pushed and pulled and heaved.

"This *is* heavy," said Mr. Sherwood. "No wonder the boys couldn't lift it."

Finally the trunk was freed and two men started down the path with it. Then they paused and one turned back to ask, "How do we get out of here anyhow?"

"Abner, lead the way," said Mr. Doubleday.

Abner, Hans, and Charley ran on ahead. When they were a little distance ahead of the men, Charley whispered, "I was scared. Were you?"

Abner didn't answer for a moment. He was thinking of the still woods and the dark shadows and the worrisome little sounds. Then he nodded. "I was scared, too, Charley."

The three boys and the men with the trunk made quite a parade as they entered the stage office. Everyone on Genesee Street stopped to ask what had happened. The three boys were heroes.

The biggest surprise of all came when Mrs. Taylor was told that her trunk was found. She was delighted and promptly said, "Mr. Sherwood, I would like to reward the boys." Then she reached into her silk bag and pressed a shiny half dollar into each boy's hand.

Three Old Cat

ALTHOUGH supper was over, the day was still bright. The hot August sun sinking in the west looked orange and heavy and the grass was brown and dry.

Father stood on the veranda with one foot on the porch railing and looked at the western sky with a thoughtful expression on his face. Abner and Tom were rolling and wrestling in the yard, and Ulysses was playing with Brownie.

Presently Mother and Amanda came from the house to the veranda. They had been washing the evening dishes, and Mother was still rubbing her hands to dry them.

"How would you like to sit under the oak tree, Hester?" Mr. Doubleday asked. "There should be a fresh breeze there."

Mother smiled. "That should be very nice."

Father carried two rocking chairs from the veranda to a spot under the big oak tree. The shiny green leaves rustled slightly in the faint summer breeze.

Amanda brought her doll and doll clothes and sat on the grass at Mother's feet. She cuddled the doll in her arms and rocked her gently. She was very proud of Martha Ann Susan. Father had brought the doll all the way from New York City. Her shiny black hair was painted on in bumpy waves, and her face was white with a delicate pink mouth. Her painted blue eyes stared up at Amanda without changing.

Ulysses ran past Amanda and Brownie jumped over her lap to catch him.

"Ulysses, stop it!" Amanda cried. "Brownie

almost landed on Martha Ann Susan!" She looked at her mother appealingly. "Make him stop, Ma!"

"You and Brownie sit down and rest for awhile," Mother said. "It's too hot to run so hard." She rocked back and forth with an even motion, fanning herself with a paper fan.

Ulysses went over and sat down beside Abner and Tom, who were leaning against the tree.

Brownie lay in front of the boys with his eyes on them. He put his head down on his front paws and lay panting.

"Want to see my silver half dollar, Tom?" Abner asked. He held the coin in his hand as he admired it.

Tom drew down the corners of his mouth. "I've already seen it!"

Abner shrugged. "Want me to tell you how I got it?" he went on.

"I know," Tom said flatly. "You've told me

before." He got to his feet. "Why don't we get some of the boys and play ball?"

"All right, let's!" Abner put his half dollar in his pocket and scrambled to his feet. "I'll go get Charley and Hans."

"I'll go over to the school yard. Maybe I can find John and Jake and Will there."

Brownie leaped to his feet and stood with his tail wagging, waiting to go with the boys.

"We'll play here in the field," Tom said and started to run, with Brownie at his heels.

Mother shook her head. "Abner—Tom—isn't it very hot to play ball?"

"Oh, Ma, it's never too hot to play ball!" Abner said.

Pa laughed as he wiped his face with a large white handkerchief. "You see, Hester!"

"Pa, will you call Brownie," Tom yelled from the path. "We can't play ball with him."

"All right, Tom." Pa called Brownie, who

came back slowly and reluctantly to sit beside Mr. Doubleday's chair. Pa put his hand on Brownie's head, and Brownie looked up at him and then at the running boys. There was a puzzled look in the dog's eyes. He couldn't understand why he couldn't go, too.

Pa laughed. "It's all right, boy. You stay here and keep cool. You can't play ball because you always want to win."

Mrs. Doubleday, who hadn't been listening, said suddenly, in a serious voice, "Ulysses, do you think you'll be elected to Congress this November?"

Pa grinned wryly. "Well, since I'm a candidate for the Congress in this election of 1830, I hope I'll win."

"Ulysses, I'm serious," she said. "Do *you* think you'll win?"

Mr. Doubleday's grin disappeared and he added seriously, "Hester, I think the Jackson

Democrats will win. As a member of that party, I hope I will be elected, too."

Mrs. Doubleday nodded. "You *will* be elected, Ulysses, not because of your political party but because your neighbors and friends know you are a man of your word. They can trust you to do what you think is right."

Brownie sprang to his feet and started to run. "Wait a minute, boy!" Mr. Doubleday reached out and caught the dog. Brownie lay down again, but whined pathetically when he heard the boys returning.

"THAT'S THE GAME!"

Abner, Charley, and Hans laid out the ball field. "That tree will be the goal," yelled Abner. He threw down a rock. "This will be the hitter's rock." Then he paced across the field to a spot about halfway between the two points and

128

crossed two sticks on the ground. "This will be where the tosser stands."

Just then Tom and his friends came running up. "What are you doing, Abner?" asked Tom.

"Just laying out the field," Abner told him. "This is the tosser's spot and that tree is the goal——"

"Aw, that's not far enough," said a boy named Jake. "Make it the next tree."

"That's not fair!" shouted Charley. "You're bigger than we are!"

"What's wrong, Charley?" asked John in a taunting voice. "Are you too little to play?"

"Aw——" Charley began, but when John looked as if he were ready to fight, Charley turned and went over to where Abner was standing.

"How many of us are there?" asked Tom. He counted. "Six. That's enough for three old cat." He paced off to a fence post. "This will be the first goal. Jake, your tree will be the second goal, and that big rock over there will be the third goal."

Suddenly Abner felt something tugging at his pants leg and looked down. "Tom, look!" he cried. "It's Brownie again."

"Brownie, go back to Pa!" Tom scolded.

Brownie stood motionless, head down. He wouldn't look up.

"Pa! Call the dog!" Abner shouted.

Father stood up and saw Brownie with the boys. "You rascal!" he said, laughing. "Come on now, Brownie. The boys don't want you."

Brownie walked back to the tree slowly, his head still down and his tail between his legs.

"It's not that bad, Brownie," Pa said, laughing again.

With Brownie out of the way, the boys went on with the ball game. "You toss first, Jake," Tom said. "John can bat."

"I want to bat!" Abner protested.

"You can be next, then Charley," said Tom.

"I'm ready," Jake yelled.

John picked up the big flat bat and took his place at the batter's rock. "I'm ready, too."

Jake threw the ball in a high, arching pitch. John swung as hard as he could. With a sharp *crack* the ball flew over Jake's head into the field. John ran for the first goal.

"That was a good one!" Tom yelled. "Come on, Abner, you're next!"

Abner took his place at the hitter's rock while Jake came behind him to catch and Tom took Jake's place at the tosser's mark.

Abner stood waiting, bat up, ready to swing at the first good ball, but Tom didn't move. "Come on, Tom!" he called. "Toss it!"

"Hold your horses," Tom said. "I'll toss it all right, and I'll catch it, too!"

Abner grew a little tense. If he hit the ball

and Tom caught it he would be out and Tom would take his place. He straightened his shoulders and tightened his grip on the bat.

Suddenly Tom threw the ball. Abner waited, eyes following the ball, and at the right moment swung with all his strength. *Crack!* The ball sped away and Abner dropped the bat and ran for the fence post.

Just as he grabbed the post, breathless, someone shouted, "He's out!" His heart sank with disappointment. Then he heard, "Tom soaked John!" He turned to look. Tom had thrown the ball at John as John had run from the fence post to the second goal and had hit him in the leg. Any runner hit with the ball was out.

Abner jumped up and down with glee. He was safe after all! Now Tom took John's place at the second goal on the field. John went limping out to the field, with one hand on his leg where the ball had hit him.

Mrs. Doubleday stood up, frowning. "Are you all right, John?"

"Yes, ma'm, I'm all right," he said.

She turned to Tom. "Tom, I don't think you should play so rough."

"Oh, Ma, that's all right!" Abner yelled. "That's the game."

"Don't worry, Hester," Mr. Doubleday said. "That *is* the game."

She sat down again, but she still looked worried. "I don't know why they have to be so rough, though," she said.

The boys played on. They yelled and screamed. Abner ran on to the tree, then to the big rock, and finally to the batter's rock without being hit. Each of the boys got a chance to bat and toss. When they were waiting their turn they stood around trying to catch a ball so they could put the batter out.

They all had a good time. After while the sun

134

disappeared and dusk came. Shadows deepened, and the sky turned gray with the coming of night. Gradually the light of coal-oil lamps began to shine through the windows of near-by houses.

One by one the ball players were called home, and their merry shouts and yells ended for the night.

Town Ball

ABNER RAN to the woodpile to bring in a load of wood before he left for school. Though the winter chill had not left the air, he noticed, the sun was warmer and beginning to promise longer days. He rushed back into the house shouting, "Ma, it's getting warmer!" He dumped his wood in the woodbox beside the stove.

"Abner," Ma scolded, "put the wood down gently. You get dirt all over the kitchen."

"When is Pa coming home?" asked Amanda, who was sitting at the breakfast table.

"He should be home before too long," Ma answered, smiling. She looked up at the almanac calendar on the wall. "Today is the 25th of March, 1833, and he said he would be home in the spring."

"Last year he didn't get home until summertime," said Amanda. "It seems as if he's been gone forever."

Abner nodded. "He left for Washington before Christmas."

Mrs. Doubleday agreed with the children. It had been a very long time! Ulysses Doubleday had been elected to Congress from their district, just as she had known he would be. As the representative, he had been in Washington all last winter and into summer. This year he had had to leave before Christmas, and she wondered how much longer he would be.

"Is that enough wood now, Ma?" Abner asked. "May I leave for school?" He was eager to get to school because he wanted to play ball for a while before school started.

He ran all the way and when he got there he found that Charley had already arrived. "Hey, Charley!" he cried. "Toss the ball to me!"

"Do you have your bat?" asked Charley.

Abner put his books in the fence corner and tossed his jacket on top of them. Then he pulled out his small flat bat and held it up.

Charley tossed the ball easily and Abner swung at it and sent it over the fence. He ran to the fence post and back for a tally while Charley ran after the ball.

Then it was Abner's turn to throw the ball and Charley's turn to bat. While they were playing John came up. "Can I play, too?" he asked.

"Sure," Abner answered. "You can be the next hitter." He raised his arm slowly and threw the ball to Charley.

Charley bent his knees slightly and swung. The edge of his bat caught the ball and the ball went straight up, then bounced crazily to the right. Charley ran for the fence post and Abner ran for the ball, but before he reached it John picked it up and threw it to him. Abner wheeled to throw Charley out, but Charley had already reached the post.

"All right, John, you're up," Abner said.

John ran to pick up the bat. He bent over the batter's rock and looked at Abner over his shoulder. Abner acted as if he were going to throw the ball, then didn't.

John started to swing, then stopped when he realized what Abner was doing. "Come on!" he yelled impatiently. "Throw it!"

Abner threw the ball so quickly that John wasn't ready and missed it completely. Abner and Charley laughed, and some of the other boys who had gathered to watch laughed, too. John's face grew red. He didn't like to be laughed at.

"All right, what about a good toss?" he said.

Abner looked back at Charley, who was ready

to run when John swung at the ball. When Abner looked at him, Charley ran back to the post and touched it with his foot. Turning quickly, Abner threw the ball to John, who swung at it and sent it flying.

John ran for the fence post and Charley for the hitter's rock, while Abner ran back toward the corner of the yard, trying to catch the ball. Just as he held out his hands the school bell rang, and in the next instant he collided with Hans, who was running to catch the ball, too. The ball fell to the ground a few feet away. Both boys dived for it.

John ran back to the hitter's stone. "I'm safe!" he yelled happily. "Count one tally for me!"

Abner looked up. Sure enough, John had run to the fence post and back while he and Hans were trying to get the ball.

The school bell rang again. "Dong-dong! Dong-dong!" It sounded more demanding this time. This was the last bell and the boys were supposed to be inside in their seats.

Quickly gathering up their books, they ran in through the door. Mr. Hansen looked up from his desk as they slipped into their desks. They all looked flushed and hot from the game. Abner's hair was mussed and brown curls were popping up and falling down over his forehead.

Katy, the girl who sat beside Abner, giggled and whispered, "Look at the curlyhead."

Abner's face grew redder. He set his mouth in a straight line. Without even looking at Katy, he rose and went back to the corner where the water bucket was kept.

He dipped the ladle into the cool water. Then he put it to his mouth and took a drink. He was hot and dry and the cool water tasted good. As he put the ladle back he spilled some water on his hands. Then he rubbed his hands over his head to plaster the hair down.

"Abner!" Mr. Hansen's voice was firm. "Please get into your seat. You did not ask permission to get a drink."

The day passed slowly in the warm, stuffy room, but finally the bell rang again, marking the end of the school day. Jumping from their seats, the boys ran out to the yard as fast as they could, eager to get back to their game.

"THREE OUT—ALL OUT!"

It seemed that most of the boys in school were staying for the game today. Tom and John and their friends from the upper school were there. They were so big that Abner, Charley, Hans, and the other boys from Mr. Hansen's room had to fight for a chance to play. Then there were even smaller boys standing around trying to get a chance to play. The school yard was crowded with boys. Some were swinging their home-made bats to limber up. Others were playing pass, tossing leather-bound balls back and forth.

"Since there are so many of us, we'll play town ball," Tom shouted. He swung his arm to indicate all the boys on his side of the yard. "We'll be on one team, and you boys can all be on the other team."

"All right," said John, who was standing on the other side of the yard. He pointed to the gate post. "This will be the first goal. The corner fence post will be the second goal." He pointed to a tree. "That tree can be our third goal, and this post will be the fourth goal."

Abner and Charley were on Tom's side and Hans on John's side. "I'll bat first," said Abner as he picked up his bat.

"All right," John agreed. "I'll be the tosser and Jake can catch."

Abner took his place at the hitter's rock between the first and fourth goals. The rest of the boys on John's team scattered around the playing field.

John threw the ball and Abner hit it and reached the first goal safely. Charley was next at bat. He got a good hit, too, and Abner ran on to the second goal. The boys on their team jumped up and down and yelled with glee.

Tom took his place at bat. He hit the ball so hard that it rolled beyond the third goal. Adam picked it up and threw it at Abner as Abner ran for third. It hit him in the leg.

"Ouch!" Abner felt a sharp pain where the ball had hit him.

"Hooray!" shouted John. "Adam soaked Abner! That's one out!"

Abner limped over to the fence and leaned against it to watch. Charley was at the second goal now and Tom at the first. The next batter hit the ball but was tossed out or hit on his way to the first goal.

144

Now the boys on John's team were doing the yelling. George came up to bat. Charley had made it to the third goal and Tom to the second. They were both crouched, ready to run if George hit the ball.

George watched John warily. He wanted to get a good hit so that his side could score a tally. John threw and George swung his bat as the ball came down. His teammates cheered as the ball rose in a nice full arching curve.

Charley and Tom ran, trying to score, but far out in the field little Eli Huse reached up and caught the ball in the air.

"Hooray!" John yelled happily. "Three out— all out!"

A FIGHT

The teams changed sides. John got ready to bat. Tom went to the tosser's spot and Charley got behind John to catch. John hit the ball well and ran all the way to the second goal before one of the players picked the ball up. Then Hans went to bat. He hit the first ball tossed, but Tom picked the ball up and threw it at him as he ran toward first.

The ball hit him on the side of the head. "Ow!" He fell to the ground with his arms around his head and rolled back and forth, moaning.

Tom ran to his side. "Are you all right, Hans?" he asked anxiously.

"I'll get some water," said Abner, who had run in from his position in the field.

Hans sat up slowly. "I'll be all right," he said a little weakly. He shook his head gently from side to side, then took a deep breath. "That was really a wallop!"

Tom's face was serious. "I'm sorry, Hans," he said apologetically. "I didn't mean to hit you in the head."

Hans got to his feet and the game went on. By now it was late, however, and the boys were growing tired and quarrelsome. Some of the younger boys had already gone home.

John's team was leading by a score of twenty tallies to fifteen, but John wasn't satisfied. Soon it was time for his team to bat again and Adam, one of the smaller boys, picked up the bat. John took it away from him and stepped to the hitter's rock himself.

"Hey, it isn't your turn!" shouted Charley.

"You think it isn't?" John sneered.

"Yes, I think it isn't! You don't want Adam to bat because you know we can put him out!"

John's face darkened angrily and he swaggered over to Charley. In a moment the two of them were rolling in the dirt and swinging wildly at each other.

Abner tried to pull them apart. "You two spend so much time fighting we don't have time to play ball," he said disgustedly. "Come on, now, stop fighting and let's finish the game." When they paid no attention to him, he turned away. "Come on, Hans. You bat and I'll toss."

"That's right, and I'll catch," added Tom. "Charley, you get out in the field again, and John, you stand back. Let's play ball instead of fight."

Reluctantly, John got to his feet and the game went on. Evening came and the sky grew dark, but the boys who remained continued to play. Finally Ulysses came running to the field, shouting, "Abner! Tom!"

"All right, we're coming," Abner called, and Tom echoed, "Tell Ma we'll be right there."

"We got a letter!" Ulysses shouted breathlessly. "It's from Pa! He's coming home!"

Cooperstown

PA'S LETTER said he would arrive March 26th on the four o'clock stage. Abner could hardly believe it.

On the afternoon of the 26th, as soon as school was out, he ran down the stairs and out the school door. The ball players called to him as he ran across the yard. "Aren't you going to play ball, Abner?"

"Not today!" he shouted. "My Pa's coming home!" He ran home as fast as he could. When he burst into the kitchen Ma was all dressed up in her black Sunday dress and bonnet.

"Hurry and wash your face, Abner," she said.

"Put a little water on your hair and brush it down." She looked out the door. "Good! Here comes Amanda."

Amanda entered the kitchen, followed by Ulysses. Ma told them to wash and tidy up their clothes so they would look nice when they met Father at the stage office.

"Where's Tom?" Abner asked as he washed his face and dried it on the towel.

"He's hitching Nelly to the wagon," Mother replied. "Come on, hurry now."

"Are we going to drive the horse and wagon?" asked Amanda in surprise.

"All of you come on." Ma hurried them out the door. "Pa will get there before we do if we don't hurry up."

"Why are we driving?" Amanda asked again.

"Oh, Amanda! Go on and get in the wagon." Ma was growing impatient. "We'll need the wagon to bring Pa's trunk home with us."

When the family reached the Exchange Hotel, Abner hopped down from the wagon. Tom tossed the reins to him and he tied them around the hitching post.

The whole family got out of the wagon and walked a little way down Genesee Street to watch for the stage. Amanda danced up and down. Ulysses held on to his brothers' hands and swung back and forth. Abner stood straight and tall, looking down Genesee Street as far as he could. At last, just as it seemed he would never see anything at all, a cloud of dust appeared far down the road.

"Look, Ma! Here it comes!" he shouted. He pointed down the road.

Soon he could see the moving forms of the horses pounding through the dust. Then they reached the edge of town, and the whole family leaned forward to watch the stage come thundering down the street.

"Pa! Pa!" Amanda and the boys shouted together when they saw their father climb down from the stagecoach.

Pa's dark eyes twinkled and he smiled happily. He stretched his arms past his children to take Mrs. Doubleday's hand.

Abner looked at his mother. He was surprised to see that her eyes were shiny with tears. Then he saw that she was smiling, too.

"Oh, Pa, it's so good to have you home!" cried Amanda as she snuggled up to him.

Pa took Amanda's hand and looked at his three sons with pride. "Washington was a very busy town, but it was lonely without all of you," he said. "It's good to be back home again."

"It's been such a long time!" Ma said with a little shake of her head.

Then they all began talking and laughing at once. The children tried to tell Father everything that had happened while he was gone.

"Mr. Doubleday, can I hand down your trunk for you?" asked the stage driver.

"We'll get it, Pa," Abner said. "Come on, Tom." The two boys went over to the stagecoach. Each of them took a handle of the trunk as the driver handed it down. With the heavy load between them, they hurried to the wagon. They set the trunk down and rested.

Abner looked up at the wagon. It seemed a long way to lift the trunk. Already his right shoulder and arm were tired from the weight.

"Tom, let's rest a little," he suggested. "Then we can lift the trunk up together."

Pa was stroking Nelly's nose. Nelly thought he had sugar for her, and turned her head to take it out of his hand. Then, finding the hand empty, she lowered her head to nuzzle in his pocket where he usually kept her sugar.

Ulysses laughed. "Nelly's glad you're home, too, Pa."

"No," Pa laughed, "Nelly just wants some sugar. I'm sorry, Nelly, but I don't have any for you now. You'll just have to wait." He walked round to the back of the wagon to Tom and Abner. "I'll help put the trunk up on the wagon. It certainly is good to have such big sons to help."

He looked at the trunk and then at the wagon. "Each of you take an end of the trunk and I'll lift the middle," he said. Bending his knees, he stooped to put his arms under the trunk. Abner took one handle and Tom the other.

"All right," Pa shouted, "heave!" Together they lifted the trunk with ease and set it into place in the back of the wagon.

SCHOOL IN COOPERSTOWN

During the next few years Mrs. Doubleday and her family met the stagecoach many times. Sometimes the trunk was loaded on the stage to take Father to Washington for the new session of Congress. At other times, the happiest times, the trunk came off the stage and Pa was home to stay for a while.

In the spring of 1835 Pa finally returned to Auburn for good. Abner was a tall boy then, nearly sixteen years old.

Pa was glad to be home to stay. He had found Washington interesting, but he had missed home and the family. He had sold his newspaper, the *Cayuga Patriot*, before going to Congress. Now he bought a book store. He enjoyed going to work in the store every day.

Abner enjoyed the store, too. He often helped his father unpack new books and place them on the shelves. He liked the smell of the store, the smell of new books.

One day Abner was perched on the top step of a ladder, putting some new books on the topmost shelves. He opened each book before he

placed it on the shelf. As he took one book from the box, he looked at the cover—*The Last of the Mohicans* by James Fenimore Cooper. He smiled and leafed through the pages with a warm, happy feeling.

He had enjoyed this book thoroughly when he first read it. He remembered sitting under a tree in the woods, reading about Hawkeye and Uncas, his Indian friend. The story had seemed so real then that Abner could almost see the Indians lurking behind the trees.

"Abner!" Pa's booming voice interrupted his thoughts.

"Yes, sir!" Abner answered, putting the book on the shelf and reaching for another one.

"If you stop to read all the books, you'll never finish." Even as he spoke, however, Pa laughed. He liked to read, too—in fact, that was one reason he had bought a book store.

"When you finish with that box of books, come

on down," Pa said. "I want to talk with you about something."

Abner placed the books on the shelf as quickly as he could. He wondered what Pa wanted to talk about. Could it be about his argument with John at the ball game? He soon would know.

When he was finished he climbed down from the ladder and went back to Pa's desk. Pa looked up from his work.

"Come over here, son." Pa rose, walked around the front of the desk and leaned against it, folding his arms across his chest and pursing his lips. "Abner, I was talking to Mr. Wright, your last year's teacher, yesterday."

Abner began to feel a little uneasy. Mr. Wright had seen Abner fighting with John yesterday. Abner knew he shouldn't fight with John, but he couldn't help it. John wouldn't play fair, and that always made Abner angry.

Abner squared his shoulders and looked up into Pa's face. Pa didn't look upset or angry. Abner cleared his throat. "Pa, I'm sorry about that fight——"

"What fight?" Pa asked.

"The one with John at the ball game yesterday. Mr. Wright saw us."

Pa's face was solemn, but his eyes twinkled. "Oh, so you were fighting yesterday! The truth will out!"

Abner felt embarrassed. He wished Pa would get on with it. Pa must not have known about the fight after all.

"Abner, Mr. Wright thinks you ought to go to another school this fall," Pa went on.

"Another school!" Abner cried. "Why?" He felt uneasy, unsettled.

"Well, it's just that Mr. Wright thinks you should go to a more advanced school to learn more than you can here," Pa explained. "I've thought a great deal about your schooling since talking with him, and I've decided he's right.

"As you know, Abner, I grew up in Cooperstown. When I passed through there on my way home I talked with my cousin Seth, who is on the board of trustees of a fine new academy there. He told me that his own sons were attending it."

Abner frowned and smoothed back his unruly hair. "You mean you want to send me to Cooperstown to school, Pa?" He didn't know whether he liked this idea or not.

"Yes, Abner, I think it would be best for you to go to the academy in Cooperstown. I mentioned it to Mr. Wright and he agrees. He feels that you could pursue your studies better there. He says you are an excellent student and would have more opportunity to learn in Cooperstown. When you finish your course there, it might be possible to obtain an appointment for you to the United States Military Academy at West Point. What do you think of that, son?"

Abner was confused. It was hard for him to think about all that his father had said. He knew about West Point. He had heard about the cadets and their handsome uniforms. If he went to West Point he would be in the United States Army. He could carry on as his grandfather Captain Abner Doubleday had done. Maybe he would become an officer himself someday.

Suddenly he realized that his father was still talking. "Cousin Seth says you may stay at his house and go to school with your cousins."

"Yes, Pa," Abner said uncertainly. "I'd like that—I think."

In a short time arrangements were made for Abner to go to Cooperstown, and Cousin Seth was expecting him. In some ways Abner looked forward to the new school. He enjoyed school. There was much that he wanted to learn, and a new school would be interesting. Besides, he was looking forward to staying with his cousins.

It was difficult for him to think about living away from home, however. He had lived in Auburn most of his life and he felt that he belonged here.

A day or two after all the plans had been made, Abner was walking down the board walk on Genesee Street, kicking his feet against the boards. He had his leather ball in one hand and his flat bat over his shoulder.

"Hey, Abner!" he heard someone shout and turning saw Charley running to catch him. "Going to play ball?"

"Yes," Abner said. "Let's go down to the field." He began to run.

"Abner, I heard my Ma say your Pa is going to send you to Cooperstown next fall for school. Is that right?" asked Charley.

"I reckon it is," Abner said slowly. His heart felt heavy.

"Will there be boys there to play ball with?" Charley asked.

"There'll be my cousins. Maybe they have some friends," Abner replied.

"What if they don't like to play ball?"

Abner frowned. What if they didn't!

The rest of the boys were already at the field. "Hurry up, you two!" they shouted. "We have enough for town ball."

TROUBLE WITH JOHN

It didn't take long to choose up sides, and the ball game was soon under way. Abner and Charley were on one side and John on the other. John was not in a good humor and yelled at Abner on the slightest excuse.

The trouble finally came to a head when Charley was at bat and John was tossing. John threw the ball and Charley swung at it and hit it high above John's head. John ran back a few paces and the ball fell into his hands. He smiled, then noticed Charley still running for the first goal. Without a pause he threw the ball at Charley as hard as he could.

Abner, horrified, watched as the ball struck Charley in the side of the head with a loud *thud*. Charley fell to the ground, clutching his head.

"*Charley!*" Abner ran across the field and threw himself down beside his friend. "Charley! Are you all right?"

Charley nodded, though he still held his head tightly. Tears rolled down his grimy cheeks, but he didn't make a sound.

The other boys gathered round. Suddenly Abner felt his face grow hot and his insides tighten up with anger. He sprang to his feet and clutched John by the shirt.

"You had no need to do that!" he cried angrily. "He was already out! You didn't need to burn him too!" He drew his fist back threateningly.

"I'm sorry," John said with a sickly grin. "You and Charley are always right. I just wanted to make sure he was really out." He shook himself free from Abner's grip.

Abner looked at him a long time, then, dropping his hand, turned away disgustedly. There was nothing to be gained by fighting. It was always this way with John. It was hard for him ever to play fair.

Baseball

FINALLY September came—September of 1835 —and it was time for Abner to go to Cooperstown. One day he went for a long walk in the woods. As he walked, he thought of all the times he had tramped along these paths.

He looked carefully at each tree as if he had never seen it before and never would see it again. Patches of pale golden sunlight trembled on the path, and the trees had the dry green look of approaching autumn.

The woods were quiet. Now and then a slight rustle betrayed the presence of animals, but Abner saw nothing.

Brownie trotted slowly at Abner's side, his fluffy tail waving gently. Brownie didn't nip at heels any more, or run and jump as he used to. He had become a settled old dog.

Abner walked on and on. Finally he came to the thicket where he and Charley and Hans had found the trunk. He sat down. Brownie sat beside him and pushed his nose under Abner's elbow so that Abner's arm was around his neck. He looked up at Abner with his soft brown eyes.

Abner patted the dog's head. His throat felt tight and dry. He remembered how Brownie had sat with him beside the trunk while they had waited for Charley and Hans to go for help. He put his face down on Brownie's head. "I'll sure miss you, Brownie," he whispered.

A few days later Nelly and the wagon took a trunk to the stage depot again, but this time it was Abner's, not Pa's.

Abner felt lonely as he bounced along in the

stage to Cooperstown. Pa's cousin Seth met him at the depot and took him home. There all Abner's cousins were gathered to meet him. Before the afternoon was over Abner and his cousin John Doubleday were out in the barn lot playing ball together.

Though Abner missed his family and friends, he enjoyed his winter in Cooperstown. He enjoyed living with Cousin Seth's family and felt at home with them. He did well at the Academy, and he liked the countryside around the town. He especially liked to walk through the woods around Lake Otsego and to stand and look at the smooth surface of the lake that James Fenimore Cooper had called Glimmerglass.

He soon found that the boys in Cooperstown liked to play ball as well as the boys in Auburn. They went to Phinney's pasture almost every afternoon for a game of town ball.

They had rollicking good ball games, too, but

the games often ended in fights because the boys could never agree on how to play the game.

When Abner took his place at bat one day, Elihu Phinney yelled to him to stand back farther.

"Yesterday afternoon you told me to stand here," Abner protested.

"Yes, but I changed the batter's stone," Elihu said. "It was too close."

"What do you mean—too close?" Cousin John demanded as he walked toward Elihu. "It wasn't too close when you were batting."

"Aw, he's just changing the rules again!" Joseph yelled from out in the field.

"Come on and throw the ball!" Abner shouted. "I'm getting tired of standing here."

The ball game went on, but each afternoon it was the same thing. The rules were changed and each player had different ideas about what they should be.

One day George made a rule that four outs instead of three would be required for a whole team to be out. On the way home after the game Abner and his cousin John talked about the game and the way the boys were playing.

"We spent the whole afternoon fighting," Abner said disgustedly. "Nobody got to play, just because George wanted to change the rules so he could bat after Elihu put Joseph out."

"Everybody knew there were three outs already," John agreed. "George wanted to change the rules to four outs so they could still bat."

"I think we need some new rules that would stay the same," Abner said. "And if we had fewer boys playing on a side, everyone would get more turns at bat."

ABNER MAKES RULES

One spring day not long afterward, Abner came to Phinney's pasture prepared with a plan.

The boys were all gathering for their usual game of town ball after school.

The air was moist and sweet. The little creek at the corner of the pasture trickled over its rocks. The trees were beginning to show the soft green of budding leaves, and though the sun was warm the earth still held the moist chill of winter not quite past.

Abner walked up to the group of boys. He took a stick and started to draw in the soft dirt at their feet. The boys watched curiously.

"What are you doing, Abner?" asked Elihu.

"I have an idea for a better way to play ball," Abner answered.

"What way?" asked his cousin John.

"Here, I'll show you." Abner drew four lines in the dirt to indicate a diamond-shaped playing field. "We'll have four bases where the batter is safe," he said, and punched a spot in each corner of the diamond.

Elihu Phinney, Nels, John Graves, and John Doubleday all gathered around Abner to watch. Seeing them, Joseph, John Starkweather, Tom Bingham, and the rest of the boys came over to see what Abner was doing.

"Where will the tosser be, Abner?" asked John Starkweather.

Abner drew a circle in the center of the diamond. "This is the place where the thrower will stand." He poked a spot behind one corner. "The catcher will stand here," he went on. Then he marked two spots within the diamond for players to stand and four places outside the diamond for the outfielders.

"There'll just be eleven players on a team, and we'll have two teams," he went on. Then, looking at George, he added, "Three outs—all out!"

"Oh, Abner, now we'll never get a chance to play!" little Tad complained. "With only eleven

174

boys on a team the big boys will never choose the little boys."

"You'll get a chance," said Abner. "Maybe some of you smaller boys can play together instead of standing around and trying to catch a ball to get a turn."

Elihu Phinney, who was one of the largest boys, shouted, "Oh, come on! Let's play town ball—the way we always do."

"Yeah, let's play town ball," echoed Joseph. "Those rules are too hard to remember!"

"They're not half so hard as remembering new rules every game we play," Abner retorted.

"Let's try Abner's game," argued Tom Bingham. "It's worth trying. Abner's right. We need some rules. We spend so much time fighting we don't have time to play ball."

"Come on!" Abner ran across the field, placing the flat stones for the three bases where the runners would be safe. "Play baseball!"

The boys did play baseball that day. They all had such a good time that the next afternoon, with very little argument, they played baseball again. The rest of that spring the Cooperstown boys played baseball in Phinney's pasture nearly every afternoon.

BASEBALL AT PHINNEY'S

One day when Abner and his friends gathered at the pasture for the afternoon ball game, Professor Green brought his team of boys to play against them. It was a bright sunshiny day—a fine day for a game.

The Professor acted as the captain of his team. "Abner," Elihu said, "you be the captain of our team and I'll pitch."

"All right, and I'll catch," Abner answered.

The boys on Abner's team scattered over the field to take their places, and the Professor's

176

team batted first. They made three runs before Abner and his teammates could put them out.

Then Abner's team came to bat. These boys played together every day. They could hit the ball, and they could run. They tallied five runs before taking their third out.

Each team had several turns at bat. Abner's team made twenty-one tallies, and Professor Green's team only nineteen.

Finally the sun began to set. It was hard to see the ball in the gray dusk, and the air was growing cool and damp. As the Professor's team came to bat, he shouted, "Whoever wins this time at bat wins the game! It's getting too late to play any longer."

Everyone grew excited. Elihu took his place to pitch. Abner crouched behind the batter to catch. The other boys on the bases and in the field jumped up and down and yelled.

Elihu tossed the ball to Phillip, Professor

Green's first batter. Phillip swung and hit the ball. He dropped his bat and ran for first base, but Nels picked the ball up in the infield and threw it at him. It caught him on the leg before he reached base.

From first base John Starkweather yelled, "You're out! You're out!"

The next batter up hit the ball into a high arc and Joseph caught it before it reached the ground.

"Two outs!" shouted Elihu. "Only one more!"

Then Professor Green picked up the short wooden bat and took his place at the home base, waiting for Elihu's pitch. Everyone grew quiet. Abner crouched low behind the base, with his eyes on Elihu. He was hot and his throat was dry. He wanted to win this game!

Elihu tossed the ball. The Professor swung mightily but missed the ball. Abner shouted gleefully as he caught it and threw it back.

Again Elihu tossed, and again the Professor swung and missed. Everyone was excited now and began to shout.

As he stooped behind the Professor again, Abner felt breathless. He couldn't help grinning. If only the Professor would miss!

Elihu waited a moment, then tossed. This time the Professor really swung at the ball, but it flew straight into Abner's hands. The Professor had missed again!

When Abner caught the ball, he leaped up and pounded the Professor on the back, shouting, "Professor's out!"

The rest of the boys on his team yelled with glee. It had been an exciting game—and all the more because Abner and his team had won.

The First Shot

EVERYWHERE Abner went he tried to get the boys to play baseball with his new rules. When he returned to Auburn, he tried to persuade his old friends to play his way.

Charley, Hans, and the others were glad to have Abner back to play with them again, but they weren't sure they wanted to change their way of playing ball.

"I don't know, Abner," Charley protested one day. "Those rules seem hard to remember."

"Charley, they're really easier," Abner said. "They're always the same. We don't get into fights all the time over changing the rules."

180

Hans frowned. "Is this the way the boys in Cooperstown play?" He wasn't so sure he wanted to play the game their way.

"Sure, and it's fun," Abner answered. Then he saw that Hans might not be willing to play if he thought the ideas were coming from Cooperstown. He added quickly, "But it was my idea, because they got into so many fights when they played town ball. I got tired of all their fights and decided to do something about them."

When the boys learned that Abner had made up the new rules, they agreed to try them. Later, even John admitted that the game was the best they had ever played.

Abner had not been home long when he left his friends to go away to school again. This time he received an appointment to the United States Military Academy at West Point. He studied hard at West Point and was graduated with the class of 1842. Upon graduation, he was given a commission as Brevet Second Lieutenant in the Third Artillery.

Abner Doubleday served in the United States Army for the next thirty years of his life. He served under General Taylor during the Mexican War, taking part in the battle of Monterey and also in the battle of Buena Vista. After the war he received a vote of thanks from Congress for his work on a claims investigation.

In 1852 he married Miss Mary Hewitt of Baltimore, Maryland, and the following year he fought against the Seminole Indians in Florida. During this campaign he made numerous maps that have since been useful to the state's cities. In 1855 he became a Captain.

Throughout these years he was, in truth, following General Lafayette's bidding to bring honor to the name of Abner Doubleday. However, he performed his greatest service during the War between the States.

On November 8, 1860, Abraham Lincoln was elected President of the United States. On December 20, South Carolina seceded.

With South Carolina out of the Union, the United States held only two small forts in the harbor at Charleston. One was Fort Moultrie on Sullivan's Island on the north. The other was Fort Sumter on a small island in the middle of the bay and commanding the whole harbor. These two forts were in the most dangerous position of any army posts in the country.

Fort Moultrie had a garrison of about eighty men, commanded by Major Robert Anderson. Captain Abner Doubleday was the second in command. As both men knew, Fort Moultrie was almost impossible to defend. Sand sometimes drifted so high outside its walls that children playing on the beach could walk right over them into the fort.

One day Captain Doubleday said, "Major, would it not be better to move the garrison to Fort Sumter? That fort is in the middle of the harbor and would be easier to defend."

Major Anderson's lean face was serious. He did not answer, but he did not forget the suggestion, either. On the night of December 26, 1860, he moved his men across Charleston harbor to Fort Sumter in rowboats.

Once settled in the fort, the men waited. Provisions grew scarce, but they held on. At one time they were almost without lights, and Mary Doubleday saw that matches and candles were smuggled to them.

At last, on April 12, 1861, the waiting came to an end. At 4:30 that morning the first guns of the Confederate batteries on Sullivan's Island and the mainland opened fire. The flashes of guns and mortars and bursting shells lighted the sky.

Slowly the sky grew lighter in the east and the sun rose out of the sea. The troops inside the fort were divided to man the guns. It was Captain Abner Doubleday who aimed the first Northern gun to return the fire. The War between the States had begun.

Four years later, on April 14, 1865, after the surrender of the Confederate States, General Abner Doubleday returned to Fort Sumter to see the flag of the United States raised above the fort again. In those four years he had fought with courage and led with wisdom in many of the battles in the war of the divided nation.

GETTYSBURG

One of the most important battles in which Abner Doubleday took part was the battle of Gettysburg. As Doubleday was leading his men the commanding officer of his corps, General

John F. Reynolds, was killed. Command of the entire left wing of the Union Army fell upon General Doubleday. He paused only a moment to reflect that the command was his. Then he moved quickly to carry out General Reynolds' decision that the Union forces must fight.

All through the day Doubleday and his men held their ground against tremendous odds. In spite of bursting shells and whining bullets, he was always at the front of his troops. He led them with courage and skill, and the men pressed forward courageously.

When night fell, many of his men had been killed and wounded by the enemy's superior fire, and he withdrew his troops to Cemetery Hill. They had suffered deeply, but their magnificent effort had given the Union Army time to prepare strong positions for itself. They had made it possible for the Union Army to achieve the final victory.

The Hall of Fame and Museum

ONE SUNNY summer morning in 1963, Mike and Johnny Palmer came with their father and mother, like thousands of other boys, to visit the Baseball Hall of Fame and Museum in Cooperstown, New York.

Cooperstown was quite different from what it had been when Abner Doubleday and his friends played ball in Phinney's pasture over a hundred years before. Now a large baseball diamond, called Doubleday Field, occupied the pasture, and each year an exhibition game was played there.

As the Palmer family approached the large

brick building, Mike said, "Dad, why is the Baseball Museum in Cooperstown? This seems like an out-of-the-way place for a museum."

"It was built here because Abner Doubleday first thought of the rules for baseball here and the first game was played here," his father told him. "That was 'way back in the 1830's."

Johnny thought about that a moment, then said, "How did the men who built the museum know about that game?"

"Back in 1907 a group of important baseball officials wanted to know just when and how the game began," Mr. Palmer replied. "After a great deal of study, they decided that Abner Doubleday invented baseball here in Cooperstown.

"About forty years later some people questioned whether Abner's game was really the first baseball game," he went on. "They thought boys in other places may have been thinking of games like baseball, too, at about the same time. However, the officials built this museum here because of the game Abner Doubleday and his friends played in Phinney's pasture."

By this time the family had reached the door of the museum.

"Come on, let's go in," said Mrs. Palmer.

Inside, Johnny and Mike enjoyed looking at all the keepsakes of baseball. They saw Babe Ruth's locker, many baseballs autographed by famous players, uniforms, bats, gloves, and balls. They also enjoyed looking at the plaques of famous players in the Hall of Fame and reading the inscriptions under them.

They saw the Abner Doubleday Baseball in a small glass case on the mantle. Over the fireplace they saw an oil painting of Major General Abner Doubleday himself, and near by another painting of a battle scene at Gettysburg.

Mr. and Mrs. Palmer stopped to look at a case in which letters and pictures of Abner Double-

day were displayed. One letter in particular caught Mr. Palmer's eye. "Look," he said, pointing to it. "This letter says that Doubleday was connected with building the first cable car in the city of San Francisco."

"What was he doing in San Francisco?"

"I believe he was stationed there after the war," Mr. Palmer answered.

"Look, Dad, what is that picture of a statue?" asked Mike, pointing.

"That's the statue of Doubleday that stands on the battlefield at Gettysburg," said Mr. Palmer. "The boy who loved baseball here in Cooperstown grew up to be a courageous man who spent his life in the service of his country."